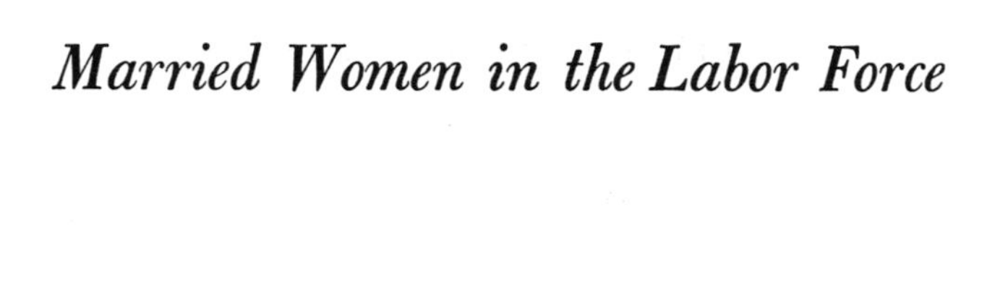

Married Women in the Labor Force

STUDIES IN ECONOMICS

of the

ECONOMICS RESEARCH CENTER

of the

UNIVERSITY OF CHICAGO

Married Women in the Labor Force

An Economic Analysis

By

GLEN G. CAIN

THE UNIVERSITY OF CHICAGO PRESS

CHICAGO AND LONDON

Library of Congress Catalog Card Number: 66-20578

THE UNIVERSITY OF CHICAGO PRESS, CHICAGO & LONDON
The University of Toronto Press, Toronto 5, Canada

To my mother

Preface

Economists engaged in research today are both blessed and cursed by a volume of data, a battery of techniques, and facilities for research that are immense and numerous. The current period in economics is, indeed, the "age of quantification" as George Stigler stated in his presidential address before the American Economic Association in December, 1964. The significance of the terms "blessed" and "cursed" are probably obvious. The research economist has in some cases inexhaustible sources of data, for as time passes and the ever growing number of survey and census data come rolling in, the sources can be literally endless with respect to one's lifetime. He has electronic computers that produce more statistical calculations than a team of researchers can digest. These represent great opportunities, but they are opportunities that can smother us in their largess, and the idea of a completed research project becomes at times mocking. One saving factor in this situation is the great increase in the number of research economists, which means that the "burdens" of the opportunities for research are, at least, being widely distributed.

The study in this book of the economic determinants of the labor force participation of married women illustrates these points. A theoretical model was developed that, however serviceable, is susceptible to many additional refinements. A large amount of data from a variety of sources was used, but only a small part of what was available at the time of my study (1962–63) and certainly a smaller part of what is currently available. The econometric or statistical techniques employed in this study, although somewhat advanced over traditional studies, are of a moderate degree of sophistication by modern standards. Moreover, the techniques used are themselves subject to any number of new and different applications—yet another variable to be added, another type of transformation or a different functional form to be tried, and so on. Finally, a growing number of economists are working on the central question of this study—the supply of labor of the household—and thus the task of reviewing the literature steadily becomes more elusive.

This book, therefore, may be considered a chapter in the ongoing research in the field. The structure of this study is such that the components complement each other, and insights gleaned from one type of data source are tested on another type of source. The most original part of the work probably lies in the analysis of the labor force participation of Negro wives (or nonwhite wives, by the census definition). But the results for this group are mainly interesting in comparison with the findings about the work behavior of white wives.

Whatever the merits of the entire study, however, the work itself would never have reached this stage without the assistance of a number of people. My greatest debt is to my thesis advisers at the University of Chicago: H. Gregg Lewis, Albert Rees, and Margaret G. Reid. I am also grateful to Arthur S. Goldberger (University of Wisconsin), to Jan Kmenta (Michigan State University), and to Robert E. Lucas (Carnegie Institute of Technology) for frequent advice during my research. Melvin W. Reder (Stanford University) read a draft of a paper based on this research that I presented to the meetings of the Econometric Society in Boston in 1963, and his comments were highly useful. Burton Weisbrod (University of Wisconsin) read portions of the manuscript and made many valuable suggestions for improvements. Finally, Marvin Kosters (RAND Corporation), whose Ph.D. thesis at the University of Chicago concerns the labor supply of married males, has been exceedingly helpful. I have benefited from his written work and also from a number of discussions with him. I, of course, take final responsibility for the shortcomings of the research.

I am indebted to the Ford Foundation for the fellowship that supported this research; also to the National Science Foundation and the Social Systems Research Institute for providing funds and services for key-punching, programming, and the use of computers at the University of Chicago and the University of Wisconsin, respectively. The Labor Workshop at the University of Chicago and the Workshop on the Economic Behavior of Households at the University of Wisconsin provided stimulating environments for this research. Finally, I owe a large debt of gratitude to my wife, Ria, for various kinds of assistance, including many hours of typing.

Contents

Contents

Tables

I

Introduction

THE FACTORS explaining market work by married women are the subject of this book. The rise over time in the work rates of wives has been impressive. The labor force participation rate of married women in the United States more than doubled from 1900 to 1940 and then doubled again from 1940 to 1960. Although the hours worked per day have decreased over time, the large rise in participation rates ensures that market work by married women has increased substantially over time. In sharp contrast are the participation rates and, more definitely, total hours of work of single women and males. Both have declined over this 60-year period, and the trends continue as of 1964 (see Table 1).

In recent years, moreover, the principal change in the composition of the labor force and the most important source of its growth has been the increased participation of married women. Between 1940 and 1960, the labor force increased by 14.4 million. The category, "married female, husband present," accounted for slightly more than 56 per cent (8.1 million) of this increase. Between 1950 and 1960 this category comprised nearly 60 per cent of the labor force growth.[1] The labor force behavior of married women over time presents a challenging problem for analysis.

There are insufficient observations from the time series, however, for statistical research, and the investigator is compelled to utilize the more plentiful cross-section data. But the economist who looks at cross-section and time series data on this problem soon recognizes a striking contradiction. First, over time the rise in income of families has been accompanied by a rise in work rates of married women, but the cross-section data show that increased income is associated with a decline in work rates. A second contrast concerns the influence of children. The most rapid increase in work rates of wives has come since 1940, during a period when birth rates have risen sharply,[2] but the cross-section relationship between the presence of children and work rates is consistently negative.

[1] U.S. Department of Labor, Bureau of Labor Statistics, "Special Labor Force Report, No. 13," Reprint No. 2364, p. 3.

[2] The number of children ever born per 1,000 women (aged 15 to 44) ever married rose from 1.9 in 1940 to 2.3 in 1959, and the rate rose for each age group of wives up to 40 years of age and older. *Statistical Abstract*, 1962, Table 61, p. 60.

Both cross-section relations, between participation rates and income and between participation rates and the presence of children, are shown in Table 2. Another interesting point demonstrated in Table 2 is that even the work rates of mothers with children under 6 years of age have increased substantially in recent years, irrespective of the income levels of their husbands.

As will be brought out in chapter 2, an enormous step in the resolution of the contradiction was taken by Jacob Mincer in a paper delivered in 1960.[3] His study, however, mainly used data pertaining to white married women for 1950, and his model did not appear to fit the data on nonwhite

TABLE 1

TREND IN LABOR FORCE PARTICIPATION RATES OF THE ADULT POPULATION BY SEX AND MARITAL STATUS

	1964[a]	Comparison I[b]		Comparison II[c]	
		1960	1940	1940	1900
Married Women	34	31	15	14	6
Single Women	41	44	48	53	46
Males	75	78	80	80	86
All Women	36	35	27	27	21
Both Sexes	55	56	54	55	52

[a] Women and men, 14 years and older. Source: U.S. Department of Labor, Bureau of Labor Statistics, "Special Labor Force Report, No. 50," Reprint No. 2457, p. 1.

[b] Women and men, 14 years and older. Source: U.S. Department of Labor, Bureau of Labor Statistics, "Special Labor Force Report, No. 13," Reprint No. 2364, p. 3.

[c] Women, 16 years and older; men, 14 years and older. Source: Clarence Long, *The Labor Force under Changing Income and Employment*, National Bureau of Economic Research (Princeton: Princeton University Press, 1958), pp. 292 and 297.

wives.[4] This latter puzzle provided the initial incentive for this study, but the range of issues expanded as the research progressed, and most of the book deals with work by all wives in the United States. The plan of this research is as follows.

In chapter 2, I present the general model developed by Mincer and discuss the modifications necessary to handle data in different forms—aggregate and disaggregate, time series and cross-section. Next, previous empirical studies are reviewed with two purposes in mind: (*a*) as illustrations of the specification of variables for the different types of data,

[3] Jacob Mincer, "Labor Force Participation of Married Women," in *Aspects of Labor Economics, A Conference of the Universities.* National Bureau of Economic Research (Princeton: Princeton University Press, 1962). See also, Mincer, "Market Prices, Opportunity Costs, and Income Effects," in *Measurement in Economics* (Stanford: Stanford University Press, 1963).

[4] "Comment" by Clarence Long on Mincer's paper, *Aspects of Labor Economics*, pp. 103–4.

and (*b*) as initial checks on whether the implications of the model are supported by the empirical results reported.

In chapter 3 the new empirical work of this research is presented and discussed. The aggregative data from the 1950 census that Mincer used are re-examined along with materials from the 1940 and 1960 censuses.

TABLE 2

LABOR FORCE PARTICIPATION RATES OF MARRIED WOMEN, HUSBAND PRESENT, MARCH 1960 AND APRIL 1951, BY PRESENCE AND AGE OF CHILDREN AND INCOME OF HUSBAND IN 1959 AND 1950

Survey Date and Income of Husband in Previous Year	All Wives 14 Years Old and Over	Wives 20–44 Years Old			
		Total	No Children under 18 Years	Children 6 to 17 Years Only	Children under 6 Years
March, 1960 Total	30	32	59	40	19
Under $2,000	30	41	54	53	29
$2,000 to $2,999	32	37	64	48	24
$3,000 to $4,999	36	37	63	49	22
$5,000 to $6,999	30	29	60	38	17
$7,000 to $9,999	25	21	51	32	9
$10,000 and over	16	15	[a]	19	8
April, 1951 Total	25	28	53	33	14
Under $2,000	29	36	55	42	21
$2,000 to $2,999	28	32	59	41	15
$3,000 to $4,999	25	26	52	33	13
$5,000 to $6,999	16	15	30	17	8
$7,000 to $9,999	7	5	[a]	4	5
$10,000 and over	12	11	[a]	11	5

Source: U.S. Department of Labor, Bureau of Labor Statistics, "Special Labor Force Report No. 13," p. 9.

[a] The number of observations is less than the minimum required for sampling reliability.

The model for the total (and, of course, mainly white) population of wives is then applied to the census data for nonwhite wives for 1950 and 1960. Next, I use two samples of survey (or disaggregated) data: the Scripps Population Foundation's Growth of American Families Study of 2,700 wives and the 1-in-1,000 sample of the 1960 census. In addition to the opportunity to check on racial differences, survey data provide independent data, consisting in a different form and derived from a somewhat different universe, with which to test the underlying general model. Another point, suggested in chapter 2, is that previous studies using survey data have not yielded very satisfactory results, and in this judgment lies another challenge.

The economic model of labor force participation of married women used in this book is tested, therefore, with cross-sectional data of two statistical types (aggregated and disaggregated), for two color groups, and from different time periods out of a span of 20 years (1940 to 1960). The evaluation of these tests made in chapter 4 involves the following three issues:

(*a*) Do the coefficients of the explanatory variables agree with the theoretical expectations, and are they consistent among the different statistical studies?

(*b*) Are the results for white and nonwhite wives compatible?

(*c*) Do these cross-sectional results conform with those from the time series?

II

The Model and a Review of the Literature

The Underlying Concepts

The study of labor force participation is a study of labor supply. The theory of labor supply is one of an individual making choices among alternative uses of his time. For present purposes it will suffice to consider two categories, work and leisure, as an exhaustive description of the choices. Work, however, may take place in the market for a money wage or in a non-market sector like the home or school. If we restrict the discussion to adults, then we might consider homework as the principal type of non-market work, and we can think of some non-money wage rate that applies to this work.[1]

For a male, homework will be a negligible part of his activities over the span of his adult life for biological and cultural reasons. The opportunity cost of not working—the price of his leisure—will then be represented solely by his market wage rate. Wage rate changes will carry both income and substitution effects on labor supplied. An increase in wages will have an income effect that is negative, since leisure is a superior good and a higher income implies that more of it will be bought, or alternatively, less time will be spent at work. The substitution effect of a wage increase will be positive since leisure time becomes more expensive relative to the alternative of work, and less leisure would be purchased.

The secular decrease in time devoted to work by males, which has been substantial, implies that the income effects have outweighed the substitution effects, given small influences from changes in institutions (like legislation), tastes, and relative prices among goods complementary to and substitutable with leisure. Furthermore, since the rises in income over time have stemmed mainly from wage and salary gains, a reasonable generalization is that the (negative) income effects of the increases in wages have swamped their (positive) substitution effects. Thus, the time series suggests that the supply curve of labor is negatively sloped.[2] This

[1] In this book homework is defined as cleaning house, raising children, and preparing meals. Child care, food preparation, and housekeeping, then, may be considered home goods.

[2] For a more complete theoretical statement of these matters see H. G. Lewis, "Hours of Work and Hours of Leisure," *Proceedings of the Industrial Relations Research Association*, 1957.

hypothesis was tested and confirmed with cross-section data in several careful studies: first by Paul Douglas and his associates, later by Clarence Long and T. Aldrich Finegan, and most recently by Marvin Kosters.[3] The "backward bending" supply curve of labor has proved to be a rather remarkably consistent aspect of behavior. Its theoretical explanation, which entails impressive empirical support, has been a noteworthy achievement of economics.

When we turn to the analysis of the labor supply of married women, the assumption that market work is the main alternative to leisure becomes inappropriate. Cultural and biological factors in this case make homework the most important type of work for the wife over most of her married life. We need to view the wife within her family context where she specializes in the production of home goods. Within this context the market and home productivities and tastes of each family member, along with the family income status, will determine the allocation among market work, homework, and leisure among all members.[4] From this point of view, let us examine the implications of the conventional theory, which had been previously applied to the individual.

For the family a rise in income should reduce the work and increase the leisure of the family members. But while the husband reduces only his market work (on the simplifying assumption that he engages in no homework), the wife reduces her homework as well. Indeed, our knowledge of the respective income elasticities of market goods and home goods suggests that homework should have declined more than market work over the long run (see p. 17).

The effect of changes in market wage rates—the substitution effect—should also be different for wives. In general, the substitution effect will be small and the supply of labor inelastic if good substitutes for one's

[3] The classic work is Erika H. Schoenberg and Paul H. Douglas, "Studies in the Supply Curve of Labor," *The Journal of Political Economy*, XLV (1937), 45–79, reprinted in *Landmarks in Political Economy*, eds. Earl H. Hamilton, Harry G. Johnson, and Albert Rees (Chicago: University of Chicago Press, 1962), Vol. I. A summary statement of Long's research is given in Clarence Long, *The Labor Force under Changing Income and Employment*, National Bureau of Economic Research (Princeton: Princeton University Press, 1958), pp. 3–7. Also, T. Aldrich Finegan, "Hours of Work in the United States: A Cross-Sectional Analysis," *The Journal of Political Economy*, Vol. LXX (October, 1962). The work of Marvin Kosters is contained in an unpublished Ph.D. dissertation, "Income and Substitution Parameters in a Family Labor Supply Model" (University of Chicago, 1966).

[4] The following two paragraphs in the text draw freely on the analysis of Jacob Mincer, "Labor Force Participation of Married Women," in *Aspects of Labor Economics, A Conference of the Universities*. National Bureau of Economic Research (Princeton: Princeton University Press, 1962).

working time are lacking. But although the substitute of leisure is available to husbands (or single men and women) and wives, the responsibilities of homework are a much more important substitute for the wife's time than for other adults. For married women, then, we should expect a relatively high elasticity for their supply curve of labor; in other words, the substitution effect should be relatively large.

The generalization that the substitution effect is large for wives and small for husbands is meant to apply to work choices in the context of a lifetime. At a particular moment in time the generalization may not hold. When young children are present, for example, the wife's time will not be easily substitutable for market work, given prevailing standards for the care of children. At other times the presence of older children or other adults besides the husband and wife, who may be productive as either home or market workers, will influence the work decisions of the wife. An even more temporary event is unemployment of the husband. This will tend to make homework a relevant alternative use for his time. But if we do summarize the lifetime experience of the family and suppress the life-cycle events or transitional situations, the generally greater area of choice between work alternatives (home and market) for wives than for husbands does imply a larger substitution effect for wives.

Herein lies the foundation of Mincer's reconciliation on theoretical grounds of the time-series differences in market labor supplied by wives and other adults. For the latter group the income effect exceeds the substitution effect, but for wives the reverse is eminently reasonable. In the face of rising incomes and rising wages market work declines for males and single women and their leisure increases, while homework declines for wives and their leisure and their market work both increase.

The Formulation for Empirical Testing

The traditional ideas of income and substitution effects provide the theoretical concepts for this study. To use the theory on actual data, however, it is necessary to devise empirical constructs of the theoretical variables and to specify a model with close attention to its functional form. It is useful to proceed in three steps: (1) a general specification of a model with a few generally defined variables; (2) a brief description of the types of data to which the general model can apply; and (3) a more exact definition and specification of the variables for the particular type of data. The third step will include a review of existing studies in the literature. The studies will illustrate statistical applications of the models developed, and the underlylng models will provide a means of evaluating the studies.

A General Model

In setting out the general model,[5] I will not at first consider how accessible the variables are for purposes of measurement. This problem is immediately seen to be serious, however, and some drastic simplifying assumptions are employed to yield more manageable models. In the discussion that follows, capital letters indicate general concepts. Lower-case letters are reserved to designate a specific measure of a general concept.

Let M be market labor supplied by the wife. This is the dependent variable to be determined by:

Y_f family income, defined as the return on the non-human capital of the family plus the maximum wage and salary earnings available to the family. It is thus a potential income concept.

W_m a market wage of the wife determined by her market skills and the market demand for those skills.

W_h a home wage of the wife determined by her home skills and the family demand for those skills. The family demand will be based on the family's income and tastes for home goods.

O_m a market wage of other family members (not including the wife).

O_h a home wage of other family members (not including the wife).

T_m the wife's tastes for market work relative to homework and leisure. The allocation of the wife's time between homework and leisure would involve a "tastes for homework" variable, but, given T_m, this should not affect M.

V an error term including other factors such as the tastes for work by other family members and prices for such relevant commodities as domestic service, restaurant meals, capital goods used in the production of home commodities, rents of dwelling units, and so forth.

Ideally, the income figures should be net of taxes that are not offset by governmental services and the wage should be net of taxes, of the expenses of working, and of non-pecuniary aspects. Even if we waive these problems, the above list of determinants for the supply of market labor of the wife obviously includes too many unobservables to be applicable to actual data. As a first step in simplifying the problem, I make the following restrictions and assumptions:

(*a*) Restrict the model to those husband-wife families with no other adults present. Thus, I need not consider cases of, say, grandmothers whose O_h is relatively high and O_m low, or male boarders whose O_m is high and O_h low. O_m is now replaced by Y, the husband's market wage. O_h will be dropped on the assumption that all husbands have the same home productivity.

[5] The model generated in this section has been more generally and more elegantly derived from the Slutsky-Hicks utility maximization model of demand theory by Marvin Kosters in his unpublished dissertation, "Income and Substitution Parameters in a Family Labor Supply Model."

(*b*) The restriction on family type made in (*a*) permits Y_f to be defined as $(Y_n + \hat{Q}Y + \hat{M}W_m)$ where Y_n is the return on non-human capital and $\hat{Q}Y$ and $\hat{M}W_m$ are the husband's and wife's potential wage and salary earnings, obtained by multiplying the quantity of work supplied by the husband ($\hat{Q}$) and the wife ($\hat{M}$) by their respective wage rates. The quantities of labor, $\hat{Q}$ and $\hat{M}$, are to be viewed as fixed, equilibrium values that: (1) are set in a way that takes into consideration the "well-being" (earnings, health, etc.) of the family members over their life span, and (2) are determined once the wage rates, property income, homework demands, and tastes of the family are known.

(*c*) The variable associated with the production of home goods by the wife, W_h, is unobservable. To get some control over the variations in the family's demands for home goods and the skills of the wife in homework, I employ a new variable, C, to represent the presence of children. With more children, especially those under school age, more homework is demanded and the higher, other things equal, is the home wage of the wife.[6]

Even if we accept C as a good measure of the amount of the wife's homework, however, there are several difficulties in the use of this proxy. In the first place we are mixing together the separate factors of her home skills and the family's (wife's included) tastes for homework and home goods. It is not hard to think of situations in which we would like to assess the separate effects of these two determinants of the home wage rate. More serious, in some contexts, is the presence of simultaneous determinations of M and C through the independent variables, Y_f and W_m. This problem is not directly confronted in this study. The statistical results are based on the assumption that the number of children per family is "unplanned." Planning would take into account family income (Y_f) and opportunity costs (W_m).[7] In a cross-section analysis the assumption may be justified on less restrictive grounds: that fertility is a "predetermined variable" that is "exogenous" to the family during the period in which the decision to work is made.[8]

(*d*) The variable representing children offers some control over tastes for homework, but there remain variations among wives in tastes for market work. (Leisure, of course, is the third alternative.) At several points such proxies as age and tenure status (renting or home ownership)

[6] It seems reasonable to assume that the amount of housecleaning and food preparation, as well as child care, will be proportional to a measure of the number of children.

[7] Birth control knowledge and family planning may themselves be related to Y_f and W_m, however, through their relation to the educational attainments of the husband and wife.

[8] For precise definitions of "predetermined" and "exogenous" variables, see Arthur S. Goldberger, *Econometric Theory* (New York: John Wiley and Sons, 1964), pp. 294–95.

are used, but for the most part tastes for market work will be unmeasured and caught in the error term. I will assume that they are uncorrelated with the other independent variables, although with some types of data variations in tastes are probably minimal, so that the problem of intercorrelation may not arise.[9]

The foregoing restrictions and assumptions permit an abridgement of the model as follows:

	Expected Effect on M
Y_f becomes $Y_n + \hat{Q}Y + \hat{M}W_m$	Negative
W_m stays W_m	Positive
W_h becomes C	Negative
O_m becomes Y	Negative
T_m stays T_m	Positive

If we stipulate a linear relation (and write W_m as W, T_m as T) we now have Model I:

$$M = a_1(Y_n + \hat{Q}Y + \hat{M}W) + a_2Y + a_3W + a_4C + a_5T + V$$

or

$$M = a_1Y_n + b_1Y + b_2W + a_4C + a_5T + V \tag{1}$$

where

$$b_1 = (a_1\hat{Q} + a_2) \tag{2}$$

$$b_2 = (a_1\hat{M} + a_3) \tag{3}$$

The interpretation of equations (2) and (3) is as follows:[10] the coefficient, b_1, of the husband's wage contains an income effect, $a_1\hat{Q}$, and a cross-substitution effect, a_2; both are expected to be negative. The cross effect stems from the likelihood that some (although probably small) alteration in the division of market labor supplied by the household will be made between the husband and wife as the husband's market wage varies, *ceteris paribus*. The coefficient, b_2, of the wife's earnings similarly contains an income effect, $a_1\hat{M}$, presumed negative, and a substitution effect, a_3, which, as an own-price effect, is expected to be positive.

The use of equations (1)–(3) to obtain precise estimates of a_1 and a_3 is beset with many difficulties. If a_3, the pure substitution effect, is to be obtained, we need to know the effect of a change in the wage rate of the wife, holding income constant—that is, the effect when the family income is compensated (raised or lowered) to just offset changes in income that result from changes in the wife's earnings. In fact, I will assume that such

[9] See Appendix C for a discussion of tastes and attitudes in the study of the labor force participation of married women.

[10] The following several pages draw heavily upon the work of Kosters.

compensation in family income occurs only by changes in non-labor income, Y_n. This avoids problems of re-introducing price effects that are inherent in the variables, W_m and Y, that determine Y_f.[11] The income-compensation adjustment will depend on what fractional part the wife's earnings are of total family income, $\hat{M}W/Y_f$. These considerations are most clearly shown in elasticity terms.

Use equation (3) and write:

b_2 as $\frac{\partial M}{\partial W}$, the change in labor supplied by the wife with respect to the uncompensated change in the wife's wage

a_1 as $\frac{\partial M}{\partial Y_f} = \frac{\partial M}{\partial Y_n}$, the change in labor supplied with resepct to changes in income

a_3 as $\frac{\partial M^s}{\partial W}$, the change with respect to an income-compensated change in the wife's wage

Then

$$\frac{\partial M}{\partial W} = \frac{\partial M^s}{\partial W} + \hat{M} \frac{\partial M}{\partial Y_n}$$

To derive elasticities, conventionally denoted by the symbol η, multiply through by W/M and divide the last term by Y_n/Y_n.[12]

Then

$$\eta = \eta^s + \frac{W\hat{M}}{Y_n} \eta_{Y_n}$$

in conventional symbols or

$$b_2' = a_3' + a_1' \left(\frac{W\hat{M}}{Y_n}\right) \qquad (3')$$

where b_2', a_3', and a_1' denote elasticity measures, respectively, of b_2, the coefficient of W, a_3, the pure substitution effect of W, and a_1 the income effect measured by non-labor income. Similarly

$$b_1' = a_2' + a_1' \left(\frac{Y\hat{Q}}{Y_n}\right) \qquad (2')$$

[11] To anticipate, this restriction derives from the inability of the single-equation specification of this model to incorporate the full simultaneity of decisions of market work by the wife and husband. This point is discussed again at the end of this section.

[12] The conversion from income elasticities in terms of Y_f to Y_n is straightforward. Multiply both sides of $\partial M/\partial Y_f = \partial M/\partial Y_n$ by Y_n/M and then multiply the left side by Y_f/Y_f. We obtain:

$$\eta_{Y_f} \left(\frac{Y_n}{Y_f}\right) = \eta_{Y_n}.$$

In principle we can derive the pure substitution effect, a_3', of a change in the wife's wage on her market labor supplied from the relations shown in (3′)

$$a_3' = b_2' - a_1'\left(\frac{W\hat{M}}{Y_n}\right) \tag{4}$$

where b_2' is observable as the elasticity coefficient of the wife's wage and a_1' is obtainable as the elasticity coefficient of Y_n. The amount of earnings from full-time work (50–52 weeks a year, for example), will approximate $W\hat{M}$ and $Y\hat{Q}$. (In practice, elasticity coefficients will be the coefficients of the logarithms of the variables.)

Unfortunately, data for income from non-wage and salary sources is often not available and when available is customarily believed to be inaccurately reported. Furthermore, even if Y_n was known and error free, several ambiguities would be present. Some forms of Y_n, such as inheritances and annuities, are by and large unrelated to work behavior, except in their role of income, per se. This is the ideal concept of Y_n. Other forms, such as rental income from boarders or tenants, entrepreneurial income, or even income obtained from the stock market are in part a return on labor—"wages" that are not reported as wages by our methods of collecting income data. Still other forms of Y_n are paid to individuals because they are not in the labor force; for example, disability insurance, workmen's compensation, and certain types of relief payments. All these types of Y_n may be expected to operate in different ways upon the decisions to work, and without more information about the composition of Y_n, it is very difficult to interpret this variable.

A second alternative for estimating income and substitution effects from the model above is to work with the observed coefficient of husband's income. Subtracting the observed elasticity of the husband's wage variable from the observed elasticity of the wife's wage we have:

$$b_2' - b_1' = a_3' - a_2' - a_1'\left(\frac{Y\hat{Q} - W\hat{M}}{Y_n}\right)$$

from (3′)–(2′). Here, only if the cross effect, a_2', of the husband's wage on the wife's labor supply is zero and the share of income earned by the wife equals the share of income earned by the husband (given $a' = \eta_{Yn} \neq 0$) will we obtain a true measure of a_3'. If the cross effect is zero, however, then by (2′) we can obtain an alternative estimate of the income elasticity; namely,

$$a_1' = b_1'\left(\frac{Y_n}{Y\hat{Q}}\right)$$

which can be used in (3′) to obtain a_3' as follows:

$$a_3' = b_2' - b_1' \left(\frac{W\hat{M}}{Y\hat{Q}}\right) \qquad (5)$$

An additional problem with equations (4) and (5) is that there is variation across observations in the weights (that is, income shares) attached to the income elasticities. This violates the assumption of constant or parameter values for all coefficients in the regression model. This problem is taken up again in chapter 3 when empirical estimates of the income and wage effects are computed.[13]

CONCLUDING OBSERVATIONS ABOUT THE GENERAL MODEL

The model developed for regression analysis in this section is given as equation (1) on page 10. Its limitations are numerous. As often happens with an attempt to specify an economic model with some rigor, the outcome reveals the formidable complexities of the problem and the somewhat discouraging restrictions necessary to make the model manageable for empirical work.

At this stage of the study these restrictions may be grouped into four categories. The first is the limitation of the model to only those families with no other workers (market or home) except the husband and wife. In addition, we assume that the home productivities of husbands are unvarying or vary in a manner unrelated to the included explanatory variables. A similar assumption would be necessary concerning the home productivities of wives unless we accept C, the measure of the presence of children, as a suitable proxy for the home productivity of the wife.

Second, the number of variables that has been left out and that might reasonably affect the supply of labor of the wife is about as large as our imagination permits. Certainly there are contexts in which there is variation in prices of domestic service and housing, of leisure goods, of payments for unemployment, retirement, or relief, and, perhaps most important, of "tastes" variables (for all family members). The assumption that these omitted variables are uncorrelated with the included explanatory variables may be a strong one.

Third, the measures of the variables that are included are admittedly imperfect. A money wage without adjustments for taxes, expenses of work, and non-pecuniary aspects is simply not the wage that economic theory would have us adopt. Similar criticisms could be made of the other variables.

[13] I am indebted to Marvin Kosters for guidance on this point.

Finally, the structure of the model implies that the wife's decision to work is influenced by the husband's earnings and the number of children, but that "causation" does not run the other way. This also is a falsification of reality. The wife's market activity probably does affect both the amount of her husband's earnings and the number of children she bears. An improved model for analyzing the labor supply of the wife would involve several equations in which, for each family member, the quantities of market work and homework (including the number of children) would appear on both sides of a system of simultaneous equations. I am not aware of any models for family labor supply decisions that are cast in such a system. A specific consequence of my avoidance of the simultaneity problem was the use of non-labor income (Y_n) to capture the "income effect." This is particularly unfortunate since Y_n is a minor component of income and especially subject to errors of measurement. A fully specified model would be able to use the variable, family income (Y_f), properly defined.

Despite all of the limitations listed above, I believe there is a large amount of information that can be learned with the use of the model that has been developed here. Further discussion of its strengths and weaknesses will arise as particular empirical applications of the general model to different sets of data are undertaken. The next section discusses the different types of data to which the model may be applied.

Types of Data

The available data can be classified into four types: aggregative data in a time series, aggregative cross-section data, and disaggregated (or individual) survey data for cross-sections and for time series. The first type is usually in the form of decennial or annual national statistics. The second is exemplified by statistics for cities or standard metropolitan areas, usually for a census year. The third type is found in the surveys of individual households, and the fourth is the uncommon panel study.

A Discussion of Applications of the Model with Examples from the Literature

Time Series of Aggregative Data

The small number of time series observations does not permit a direct statistical application of Model I. The quantitative studies that have been made are more descriptive than statistical (in the formal sense), and the best of these are enlightening.

One important finding that was initially suggested by the work of

Durand[14] and Wolfbein and Jaffe[15] is that demographic factors account for very little of the rise in labor force participation of married women over time. Later studies by Lebergott, Haber, and Long reach essentially the same conclusion.[16]

Durand examined the increase in labor force participation of women between 1920 and 1940. He determined that almost none of the increase could be attributed to the combined effects of changes in the following demographic variables: nativity, age, farm and non-farm residency, marital status, and dependency (defined as one or more children under ten years of age in a family). Wolfbein and Jaffe adjusted the 1930 population according to the age, color, and nativity composition of 1890 and found that the adjusted labor force participation rates of women for 1930 were lower than the actual rates. The adjustment not only failed to explain any of the increase, it made the increase to be accounted for even larger. Stanley Lebergott reviewed the studies of Durand and Wolfbein-Jaffe, added more data from recent years, and also concluded that demographic changes have been a negligible factor in the long-run rise in work rates of wives.

Let us draw on these studies and examine the separate effects of the demographic factors, first in the period from 1890 or 1900 to 1940. Changes in the age, color, and nativity composition of the female population operated to lower labor force rates. The proportion of the aged, of whites, and of the native-born among married women increased in this period, and all have lower rates of labor force participation than their counterparts. Changes in the proportion of farm residents and in fertility rates operated to raise work rates of wives in the period up to 1940. The urbanization and the decreased birth rates that occurred during this period induced higher work rates among married women.[17]

[14] John D. Durand, *The Labor Force in the United States, 1890–1960* (New York: Social Science Research Council, 1948), p. 67.

[15] Seymour L. Wolfbein and A. J. Jaffe, "Demographic Factors in Labor Force Growth," in *Demographic Analysis*, eds. Joseph J. Spengler and Otis Dudley Duncan (New York: The Free Press, 1956), pp. 492–96.

[16] Stanley Lebergott, "Population Change and the Supply of Labor," in *Demographic and Economic Change in Developed Counties*, National Bureau of Economic Research (Princeton: Princeton University Press, 1958), pp. 377–422; S. Haber, *Female Labor Force Participation and Economic Development* (Los Angeles: RAND, 1958), Monograph P-1504; Long, *The Labor Force under Changing Income and Employment.*

[17] One might wonder why higher labor force participation rates are associated with urban, compared to farm, residency. The explanation of this well-established association demonstrates again the wisdom of drawing a distinction between home and market work, for it is doubtful that the total amount of work by farm wives is less than that by city wives. The published statistics simply reflect more market work by city wives; hence their higher work rates.

Note that age, color, and nativity are all factors over which the individual has no control. No choices are involved, and, thus, the factors are noneconomic. But the second group of factors, fertility and residency, are very much subject to the decisions of individuals. These decisions, then, should in part be determined by economic forces. Indeed, it is likely that the same set of forces affecting labor force participation have affected fertility and residency. For example, a high wage rate that attracts wives into the labor force may also lead to birth control and limitations on family size. The migration from farms to cities was probably also induced by higher wages stemming from increased employment opportunities in the cities. There are, moreover, reasons why urbanization leads to decisions to decrease the number of children—the higher cost of children in the cities and the diminished employment opportunities for children. It would be misleading, then, to look upon the limitation of family size and urbanization as two independent and causal influences on the rise in market work by married women.

The positive relation between fewer children and work by wives does not extend, as a gross relationship, into the recent period beginning in 1940. The increase in labor force participation of married women in the last 20 years in the face of rising birth rates makes the over-all effect of demographic factors even weaker than in the earlier period up to 1940.[18] Moreover, this rise in fertility is mainly attributable to more wives bearing children.[19] It is likely that this sort of change would lower the over-all work rate of married women to a greater extent than if the larger number of children was the result of more births per mother. One final point: the timing of births in the life cycle of the family has changed over time. Wives now have their last child at younger ages, which permits a longer span of potential working years when no young children are present. But this change seems too small to account for the great increase in work rates. Glick estimates that the median age of the wife at the birth of her last child was 26.1 in 1950, 27.1 in 1940, and 31.9 in 1890.[20]

Up to now the discussion has emphasized factors that are customarily grouped under the "supply" heading. On the "demand" side, Haber stressed the changes over time in the industrial and occupational composition of the work force as the reason for increased employment of women. But most of these changes will be reflected in a rising wage rate, the W of

[18] This weakness is documented by the more recent studies of Long, *op. cit.*, and Haber, *op. cit.* See also footnote 2, p. 1.

[19] W. H. Graybill, C. V. Kizer, and P. K. Whelpton, *The Fertility of American Women* (New York: John Wiley and Sons, 1958), p. 370.

[20] Paul C. Glick, *American Families* (New York: John Wiley and Sons, 1957), p. 54.

Model I (page 10). For example, the decline in the demand for miners and the increased demand for typists will raise the relative wages of females. The wage rate is a much easier variable to handle in a statistical study and can be tied in more closely to price theory. It does fail, however, to pick up some of the non-pecuniary "wage" gains in the form of lighter and more pleasant work associated with the rise of white collar occupations and other industrial changes.

Long also discussed the shifts to lighter work that resulted from technological and demand changes, but his most impressive quantitative effort was in measuring the reduction in homework by wives. A number of his tables demonstrate the labor-saving mechanization of the home and the shift to market purchases of goods and services formerly produced in the home, all of which implies a reduction in the wife's home wage relative to other prices.[21] This research convincingly reveals the direction of these technological effects, although their reported magnitude is not large.

In addition to the findings of Long concerning the impact of technological changes, one can make a strong case for the shift over time from home goods to market goods by stressing the effect of income changes. We might make an analogy with the experience of agriculture in developing economies. Here, the relatively low income elasticity of food would decrease the share of expenditures going to agriculture over time (as national income rises), even if its relative price remained the same. To shift to our problem, assume that the economy is divided into a home goods sector and a market goods sector. Then if technological advances in the home[22] keep at parity the relative prices among home goods and market goods, the hypothesized shift to market goods would depend upon a lower income elasticity of the home goods. A large body of evidence about the low income elasticities of children[23] and food suggest that the elasticity of home goods is low.[24] Since demands for homework and market work are derived from the demands for goods out of the two "sectors," the shift from work in the home to work in the market follows from this analysis.

[21] Long, *op. cit.*, pp. 117–32. The possibility that the shift to market goods and the adoption of labor-saving devices in the home result from rises in the home wage of the wife is too far-fetched to be considered.

[22] The technological advances are assumed to be as labor-saving in the home as in the market in this brief discussion.

[23] With respect to number of children much of the evidence points to a negative income elasticity.

[24] Again: raising children, cooking meals, and housecleaning are considered the main components of home goods. Concerning housecleaning, there is evidence that the demand for numbers of rooms does not rise rapidly with income. See Margaret G. Reid, *Housing and Income* (Chicago: University of Chicago Press, 1962), p. 348.

In examining the time series of labor force participation rates of married women the investigator is usually on the lookout for those events and trends that promote work by wives, since it is the increase that calls for an explanation. For this reason one may have the tendency to exaggerate the importance of some of these events and to overlook some that operated in the other direction. For example, it may be surprising that the large advance over time in the educational attainment of youth (and the accompanying governmental provision of babysitting services) has probably not contributed much toward more work by wives in recent years. The reason is that the greater part of the high rates of school attendance among children under 13 years of age were attained several decades ago. By 1920 about 80 per cent of children of elementary school age were attending school; the increase by 1940 was only to 84 per cent, and by 1950, to 86 per cent.[25]

Similarly, it is somewhat surprising to discover that the recent popularity of nursery schools apparently has had little effect on the increase in work by mothers. A survey by the Social Security Administration in 1958 found that only around 2 per cent of the children under 12 years of age whose mothers work receives group care away from home.[26] (Group care includes day nurseries, day care centers, settlement houses, nursery schools, and the like.) It would seem that nursery schools, like domestic help, is a service that is purchased mainly among the higher income families where work by wives is much less frequent. It might be added, however, that even if a large number of the children of working mothers attended nursery schools and if the percentages had increased, this might merely reflect, rather than be the cause of, the increased labor force participation of wives. The issue would largely turn on the extent of change in the relative prices of nursery schools or the extent to which technological innovation had improved the nature of the service. To illustrate: more restaurant lunches reflect work by wives; TV dinners and frozen foods have probably contributed to causing the increase in work by wives.

One trend that began in the 1940's and that is, in principle, an im-

[25] *Historical Statistics of the United States*, Bureau of the Census, U.S. Department of Commerce, p. 214. The exact figures for 1920, 1940, and 1950 are 79, 84, and 86 per cent, respectively, but these are probably underestimates. The same table shows that the Current Population Survey reported a 93 per cent attendance figure in 1950 (compared to the 86 per cent of the decennial census survey), and Beverly Duncan used data on native males, alive in 1960, to calculate that approximately 92 per cent of those 12 years old in 1920 achieved a grade school education. Beverly Duncan, "Dropouts and the Unemployed," *Journal of Political Economy*, LXXIII (April, 1965), 121–34. These percentages are for the United States as a whole and would certainly be higher if restricted to urban areas where market work by wives is most important.

[26] Henry C. Lajewski, "Working Mothers and Their Arrangements for Care of Their Children," *Social Security Bulletin* (August, 1959), pp. 8–13.

portant discouragement to work by wives is the relatively high income tax. Since we often think of the wife's earnings as an "extra" added on to the base of the husband's, we might think that the sharp incidence of the marginal rates would be a deterrent to her working. Despite the progressive income tax, however, work rates of wives have risen rapidly and steadily since 1940. A possible explanation for the apparent minor effect of the tax system is that family work decisions of the wife and husband are sufficiently planned and integrated over the span of married life so that the wife's earnings are not, in fact, considered marginal earnings. The model of labor supply of the wife used in this book will make this simplifying assumption; namely, that income tax rates apply symmetrically to both husband's and wife's earnings, and that this rate is proportional to family income.

Cross-Section Aggregates

The application of Model I to aggregative, cross-section data will mean in this study applying it to aggregations of wives over some area, mostly standard metropolitan areas or cities. Recall that Model I was of the form:

$$M = a_1 Y_n + b_1 Y + b_2 W + a_4 C + a_5 T + V$$

The dependent variable, M, will be the labor force participation rate of the area. It is assumed that participation rates will reflect, say, hours worked per year, or a similar concept that closely approximates the supply-of-labor variable of economic theory. The following discussion of the independent variables brings out several advantages in using cross-section aggregates of areas.

The troublesome variable, tastes for market work, probably varies only slightly across these areas, so it may be dropped from the model (see Appendix C). It is helpful that variations in tastes for home goods by families (which affect the home wage) are largely washed out also, since they are undoubtedly only partly accounted for by the variable measuring the presence of children.

An obtainable proxy for family income exclusive of the earnings of the wife is the median income earned by husbands in the area, supplemented in some cases by data on average income from non-wage and salary sources. These represent an income concept relatively free of transitory or error components and closer to a "permanent" or "normal" income concept.[27] It is a long-run concept of income and appropriate to the assessment of the income effect over time.

[27] The concepts of transitory and permanent income stem from Milton Friedman, *A Theory of the Consumption Function* (Princeton: Princeton University Press, 1957). See Mincer's use of these concepts in "Labor Force Participation of Married Women," pp. 69 ff.

The median earnings of female workers provides a proxy for the wage rate facing the wife. In certain cases the earnings are based upon the sample of females who worked full-time, and this gives us a more precise measure of the wage rate, since less variation in the quantity of work will be determining earnings.

The three economic explanatory variables, Y_n, Y, and W, require additional discussion. The median earnings for both males and females in the area will, in practice, be the reported earnings for the year preceding. We could, therefore, add subscripts denoting the time period and think of the variables, M_t, W_{t-1}, and Y_{t-1}. In this manner the wage rate may be regarded as a predetermined variable and exogenous in the single equation determining labor force participation at the time of the survey.

On the other hand, if W_{t-1} is viewed as a proxy for W_t, then a special assumption must be made about the relation between M and W. Since the single equation model adopted in this study implies that the wage rate is not affected by the supply of labor of married women, the necessary assumption for the case of $W = W_t$ is that the demand for labor is perfectly elastic over the relevant range of M. The level of demand or the level of the wage rate would, under normal employment conditions, reflect the industrial structure in the particular area. A low wage level would prevail in, say, a mining community, and a high level where secretarial and professional personnel are required in large numbers. If a perfectly horizontal demand curve is a close approximation to reality,[28] we have the situation depicted in the graph below. The observed points (M_i, W_i) trace out the postulated stable supply curve. The industrial structure of the area is discussed further in chapter 3, and a simultaneous equation system that determines both M and W is briefly considered in Appendix H.

Whether the wage variable is interpreted as W_t or W_{t-1}, it is necessary to take into account the current state of the labor market. I will use the unemployment rate in the area as a proxy for current demand conditions. Assuming that $W = W_t$, the unemployment rate would then indicate the likelihood that the wife can get a job at the "going" wage. If we assume $W = W_{t-1}$, then the unemployment rate reveals the direction of the change in the wage that the wife observes in making her current decisions. If the wage rate, W_{t-1}, is assumed to be inflexible, then the unemployment rate indicates the tenor of non-wage adjustments in the terms of employment offered by employers. Specifically, Melvin W. Reder has

[28] The implication is that: (*a*) other groups (single women and males) are good substitutes in the labor force for married women, and (*b*) the fraction of the labor force that married women constitute (approximately one-sixth) is sufficiently small, so that their entrance and departure have no effect on the wage.

female

55

pointed out that hiring standards can be relaxed or tightened to change employment without altering the money wage.[29]

In principle, the female unemployment rate is the most direct modifier of *W*. As an explanatory variable, however, this unemployment rate has the defect of being part of the dependent variable.[30] In its place, the male unemployment rate will be used in the model. The latter is, perhaps, a more accurate barometer of business conditions, even as they apply to the female labor market.

The male unemployment rate will also serve in another capacity in the model. Although the median figure for *Y* eliminates much of the transitory component of male earnings found within the area, the area median itself may be abnormally high or low. One control for this is the amount of

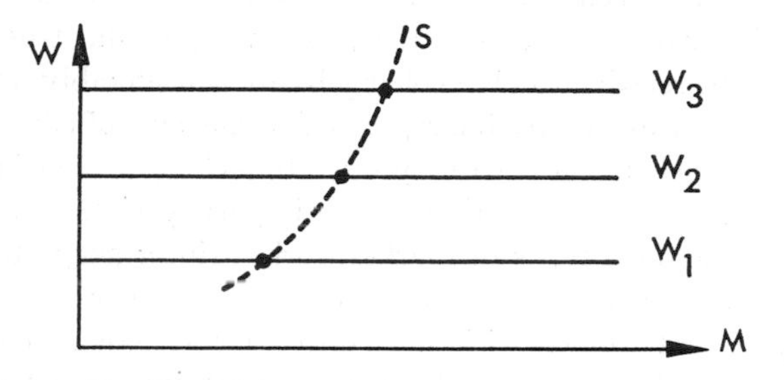

FIG. 1.—*M* is the quantity of work supplied by wives to the market; *W* is the wage offered wives; *S* is the supply curve of work by wives.

unemployment in the year for which the income is reported, but this measure of unemployment is not readily available. Again the male unemployment rate at the time of the survey can be used. How well this serves as a proxy for the amount of unemployment in the previous year is open to question. This rate should indicate, however, the effect of the current

[29] From an unpublished comment by Melvin W. Reder, who discussed a paper based on this research that I presented at the meetings of the Econometric Society in Boston, 1963. I must report, however, that Reder is far from convinced that the unemployment rate will adequately represent the effect of transitory variations in demand conditions. He suggested that the change in employment should be explicitly introduced in the model. H. Gregg Lewis later pointed out that a variable measuring "employment change" would provide a stronger test of the "added worker hypothesis" (see p. 22, footnote 31). In chapter 3, empirical results are shown that do include a measure of changes in the volume of employment where such data are available by standard metropolitan areas.

[30] Labor force participation rates are the number employed plus the number unemployed, the sum divided by the population eligible to be in the labor force. The unemployment rate is the number unemployed divided by the number in the labor force. Wives make up about one-half of the females in the labor force and about the same proportion among the unemployed.

transitory component of income of the husband on the current decision of the wife regarding labor force participation.

The unemployment rate thus plays two roles in the model, modifying both the income and the wage variables. The higher the rate of male unemployment the greater the loss in income and the greater the incentive for wives to work. But a high unemployment rate denotes a downward pressure on wages (or, alternatively, on the probability of securing a job), and lessens the incentive for wives to work. Whether the net effect of unemployment will be positive or negative is not known a priori.[31] (This problem is considered in some detail in chapter 3.)

In addition to the state of the labor market, a second characteristic helpful in interpreting the wage rate variable is the non-pecuniary aspects of the job. My own feeling is that these aspects are especially important in the female labor market, and that, for example, the true wages of white collar jobs relative to blue collar jobs are considerably understated by money wage rates. A variable representing the level of educational attainment of females in the area may serve to pick up some of these non-pecuniary aspects, since education reflects in part specialized training for the more commodious types of market work. Mincer suggested that an education variable will act as a proxy for tastes for market work.[32] It is probably true that women with such tastes would acquire more education. Some of the determinants of educational attainment are external to women, however, such as parents' income, the place and time of birth, and other similar factors.

Empirical Studies of Cross-Section Aggregates

The considerations developed in the foregoing paragraphs lead to a modification of Model I that omits T and adds variables for education and unemployment. This is the model Mincer used, except that the variable for non-labor income, Y_n, was not included. His specification for a

[31] This issue will be recognized as part of the old controversy in labor economics over the added worker hypothesis. The question of the net effect of unemployment on the labor force participation of secondary workers (like wives) has been reopened in the last few years and a number of research papers have been published. The most extensive testing has been done by William G. Bowen and T. A. Finegan, "Labor Force Participation and Unemployment," in *Employment Policy and the Labor Market*, ed. A. M. Ross (Berkeley and Los Angeles: University of California Press, 1965). For an excellent and critical review of the older literature, see Long, *op. cit.*, pp. 181–201. For an equally superb review of the more recent studies, see Jacob Mincer, "Labor Force Participation and Unemployment: A Review of the Recent Evidence," in *Prosperity and Unemployment*, ed. R. A. Gordon (Berkeley and Los Angeles: University of California Press, 1966), pp. 73–112.

[32] Mincer, "Labor Force Participation of Married Women," p. 72.

regression model using data for standard metropolitan areas (SMA's) in 1950 may be written as follows:

$$m = b_1 y + b_2 w + b_3 c' + b_4 u + b_5 e' + v \qquad (6)$$

m the labor force participation rate (in per cent) in 1950 of married women, husband present

y the median income (in hundreds of dollars) in 1949 of male family heads, wife present

w the median income (in hundreds of dollars) in 1949 of females who worked 50 to 52 weeks

c' the per cent of families in 1950 with children under 6 years of age

u the male unemployment rate in 1950

e' the per cent of population aged 25 or over in 1950 with a completed high school education or more

TABLE 3

REGRESSION RESULTS OF EQUATION (6)

	y	w	e'	u	c'	R^2
Mincer's Study						
Regression coefficients and standard errors........	−.62 (.21)	1.33 (.11)	.12[b] (.27)	−.41[b] (.53)	−.24[b] (.61)	.62 ....
Regression coefficients....	−.53	1.52	....	....	....	.51
Elasticities at means......	−.83	1.50	....	....	....	....
My Computations						
Regression coefficients and standard errors.........	−.84 (.31)	1.48 (.35)	.95[a] (.45)	−.56 (.26)	−.53 (.16)	.56 ....
Regression coefficients and standard errors.........	−.30 (.29)	1.29 (.31)	....	....	....	.38 ....

Source: Mincer, "Labor Force Participation of Married Women," p. 72.

[a] The variable e replaced e' (see text below).

[b] The coefficients are *not* significant, by the criterion of a t-value less than 1.96.

Definitions of independent variables (sources in Appendix A)

y median income for male family heads, spouse present, 1949 (hundreds of dollars)
w median income of females who worked 50–52 weeks in 1949 (hundreds of dollars)
e' per cent of the population aged 25 years and older with a completed high school education
u male unemployment rate (in per cent)
c' per cent of husband-wife families with one or more children under 6 years of age

The observations for the regression were the 57 SMA's in the North with a population of 250,000 or more.[33] Mincer's results are shown in Table 3. I also include in this table my own regression computations based on the same set of observations except for a slightly different education variable. I used e, the median years of schooling completed by females aged 25 years and older.

[33] Concerning the regional selection Mincer noted in "Labor Force Participation of Married Women," p. 72: "Southern areas were excluded because of the desire to exclude color differentials, which need to be studied separately."

The principal finding is that the effect of the wage rate is nearly twice the size of the income effect in elasticity terms. Thus, the implied large substitution effect (relative to the income effect), which was rationalized on theoretical grounds, is supported empirically—at least with this set of data. In the main, the empirical results presented in chapter 3 substantiate this finding. Another important feature of the results presented by Mincer is the insignificance of c', u, and e'; the variables for income and the wage rate provide nearly all the explanation. These results are not supported in the more extensive testing done in this study. In the light of my results shown in Table 3, which conflict with Mincer's in some respects (compare our two-variable regression results), Mincer's finding may have been the result of minor computational errors.

Two other empirical studies of labor force participation by married women that use cross-section aggregates may be discussed briefly.[34] Long computed simple regressions across cities in which female participation rates were regressed on "real earnings per adult male equivalent" for census years 1900–1950.[35] For 1940 and 1950 he tabulated percentage changes in the work rates of wives by percentage changes in 7 to 8 levels of their husband's income (Y) for several area classifications.[36] Negative relations were found in most cases. The difficulty in interpreting these results, however, is that income and substitution effects are mixed together in one variable, Y. Since Y and W are correlated, their separate effects could not be observed even in an approximate way.

In an earlier study Nedra B. Belloc correlated labor force participation rates of married women across cities in 1940 with two variables: (1) median incomes of males, and (2) the ratio of females employed in manufacturing and domestic service to all females employed.[37] The partial correlation between the labor force participation rate and the income variable was negative; the correlation between the participation rate and the

[34] The study by Bowen and Finegan mentioned previously (p. 22, see footnote 31) is omitted from this review (1) because of the lateness of my receiving the study, and (2) because it is referred to by the authors as an interim report of a larger study that will be concluded in the near future. On the basis of a preliminary publication, however, this study of the labor force participation of many demographic sub-groups of the population (including wives) promises to be a major contribution. Another study not discussed is that of Schoenberg and Douglas, but this is because female participation in the labor force rather than wives' participation was their subject. Their findings for the age groups dominated by married women are similar to those made by Long.

[35] Long, *op. cit.*, pp. 54–81.

[36] *Ibid.*, pp. 82–88.

[37] Nedra B. Belloc, "Labor Force Participation and Employment Opportunities of Women," *Journal of the American Statistical Association*, XLV (September, 1950), 401–10.

employment ratio was positive. A negative income effect is expected. Insofar as the second variable reflects an industrial structure that designates a high demand for the work of females and thereby acts as a proxy for the wage rate, the positive correlation agrees with the theoretical expectation. The choice of industries to put in the numerator of the ratio appears too arbitrary to yield a stable variable for analytical use, however.

Disaggregated Survey Data in Cross-Sections

Price theory of economics is based on the individual—person, household, or spending unit—as the unit of analysis. Our a priori predictions made about aggregations, such as those discussed in the previous section, are usually derived from what we expect numbers of individuals (as individuals) to do. Conversely, inferences made from the study of the behavior of aggregates are thought to refer to the behavior of the "typical" or "average" individual unit. At least, this is the way we customarily link price theory to the study of aggregates. Although from an empirical standpoint there are some practical advantages in using aggregations, as discussed previously, the use of disaggregated data would appear to be advantageous on theoretical grounds, since it allows us to apply more directly our theoretical models.

In several respects, moreover, this type of data provides a rich source for statistical analysis. To begin with, there are more samples that may be utilized and many more observations per sample. The smallest of the seven studies discussed below had over 400 observations. There is usually more detailed information about the characteristics of the units in the sample, which permits the use of more explanatory variables. But there are serious drawbacks as well. The advantages of cross-section aggregates mentioned previously are missing in varying degrees in the disaggregated data.

The taste factors, believed to be washed out by aggregation, are doubtless of great importance among individuals. Although the variable measuring the presence of children offers some control over differences in tastes for home goods and for homework, variation in tastes for market work is more difficult to measure. Such proxies as age, rural versus urban residency, and type of dwelling will be used, but they leave a great deal to be desired. These variables not only imperfectly represent tastes, but they partly stand for other attributes that may affect work choices. Age and home ownership, for example, may indicate an individual's wealth that is not fully represented by, say, current income. At best, we hope that our inadequate control over tastes will only lower the R^2 of the regression and leave unaffected the estimates of the coefficients of the explanatory variables.

The income variable is subject to a different problem. The wide range present is certainly advantageous to regression analysis. But the figures reported may deviate from the normal or permanent concept of income that applies to long-run behavior. To handle this problem we can, following Mincer, conceptually separate reported income into a permanent component (y_p) and a transitory component (y_t) (see pp. 27–31). The challenge is to devise means of carrying out this separation empirically. In practice, no distinction is made in measuring income by source, except to separate the wife's earnings. Thus, y_p and y_t will include the husband's earnings (by far the most important component) and, when available, income from non-wage sources (y_n). A simplifying assumption used when no data on y_n is available is that the amount is proportional to the husband's earnings.

The wage rate variable presents an even more serious problem. With aggregative data from such well-defined labor markets as SMA's, the substitution effect was represented by a market wage rate, presumed exogenous, that faced the married women. This effect now must be represented by the wage rate particular to the individual wife. What can we say about the wage rate she can earn when we have no knowledge about the prevailing market rate and no information about earnings for wives who have no jobs? Most commonly, educational attainment is used to represent earnings abilities. Two drawbacks with this procedure are that education is measured in much broader categories than earnings and that individuals with the same level of education may possess widely varying earnings capacities. These disadvantages are probably not offset by the ability of the measure for education to pick up some of the non-pecuniary aspects of the wage rate variable. When dealing with data for individuals, a disadvantage of unknown magnitude with both education and earnings is that these variables may reflect tastes for market work. Again, I will use disaggregated data and measure "wage" effects on the assumption that the absence of full control over tastes will not bias these measures.

To summarize, we can write down the following model for disaggregated data with the (tentatively) more important variables:

$$\text{Model II.}\ M = b_1Y_p + b_2Y_t + b_3W \text{ (if available)}$$
$$+ b_4C + b_5E + b_6A + V$$

Capital letters again express general concepts; the added variable, A, stands for the age of the wife.

Empirical Studies of Disaggregated Data for Cross-Sections

Most empirical studies of the labor force participation of married women have involved survey data and have used some form of regression, correlation, or variance analysis. Some were conducted by sociologists and psychologists and were addressed to such issues as wives' attitudes toward work, reasons given for working, the effects of work by the wife on family and children, and so on.[38] In this regard there appears no firm evidence of any harmful effects on the children of mothers who work.[39] A contrary finding would have implied a serious understatement in my measure of "opportunity costs" in the economic model of work by wives. Except for this finding—which I consider rather comforting in several respects—I do not believe the issues raised in sociopsychological literature are central to this study.

Seven papers by economists will be discussed.[40] The first is by Mincer who refashioned the model discussed in the previous section to handle disaggregated data, but then grouped the observations and analyzed tables of cell means to determine income and substitution effects. The other six studies used multiple regression analysis on the individual observations, and this is the technique I use in chapter 3.

Mincer's data consisted of 6,766 white, husband-wife families, excluding units of which the heads were self-employed or not gainfully employed.[41] The source was the 1950 Survey of Consumer Expenditures of the Bureau of Labor Statistics. The data on employment and earnings referred to 1949. His basic model was:

$$M_i = b_{i1}Y_{ip} + b_{i2}Y_{it} + b_{i3}W_i + V_i$$

where i refers to the group of the observations. There were 12 groupings based on the following characteristics of the husband: education (three

[38] For a substantial bibliography see Alva Myrdal and Viola Klein, *Women's Two Roles: Home and Work* (London: Routledge and Kegan Paul, Ltd., 1956); and Ivan Nye and Lois W. Hoffman, *The Employed Mother in America* (Chicago: Rand McNally, 1963). Not all the works cited are cross-section survey studies, but most of the empirical ones are.

[39] For a compact summary of this issue see, Alice S. Rossi, "Equality between the Sexes," *Daedalus* (Spring, 1964), pp. 607–52, especially p. 617.

[40] This discussion pivots around the model of labor force participation used in the text and does not purport to give a complete analysis of these studies.

[41] This research was included in the previously cited paper, Mincer, "The Labor Force Participation of Married Women." The term "head" rather than "husband" was used in Mincer's paper, but it does not seem misleading to continue to use "husband" throughout this discussion.

groups), and presence of children under 16 years old along with the age of the husband (four groups). In separating wives with children under 16 years of age from those with no children under 16, Mincer was able to check on whether the income and wage variables might affect differently the labor force behavior of the two groups. For each of the 12 cells, mean earnings of wives who worked during 1949 measured W.

Mincer first estimated the following relation:

$$m_i = b_1 y_i + b_2 w_i$$

for $i = 1, 2, 3, 4$ groups of wives (with or without children under 16 years of age; husband under or over 35 years of age).

The variables were defined as follows:

$m_i =$ the proportion of wives who worked some time in 1949
$y_i =$ the average earnings of husbands in the group
$w_i =$ the average earnings of wives who worked.

Now, within any group the husband's income is positively related to the wife's earnings. For three of the four age-dependency groups the tables showed that the positive effect on work by the wife of wages earned by the wife outweighed the negative effect of the husband's income on her work. This supported Mincer's cross-section findings with SMA data (see pp. 23–24).

The wage effect was weakest and smaller in absolute value than the income effect in the group in which young children were present. This meant that the employment rate of wives in this group with young children present was *lower* as their husbands' incomes were *higher*, despite the fact that high income of the husband was associated with a high wage (or earnings ability) for the wife. Mincer commented that the absence of good substitutes for the mother's care of small children suggests, a priori, a small wage effect (and/or a large income effect).[42] A second characteristic of this group was the lower levels of participation. In the language adopted in the initial specification of the model, we could say that the unobserved home wage was highest in these instances, thereby discouraging market work by the wives.

Secondly, Mincer attempted to determine the effect of the transitory component of income, y_t. To do this, he regressed m_i on y_i and a second independent variable, "weeks worked by the husband." The partial regression coefficient of the last named variable ($b_{me.x}$ was the symbol Mincer used) measures the effect of a change in weeks worked with total

[42] *Ibid.*, p. 78.

earnings, y_i, kept constant. The $b_{me.x}$ partials were negative in 9 cases out of 12. Mincer commented:

Now a decline in weeks, keeping total earnings constant, means a corresponding amount of increase in earning power, which is offset by a transitory loss of income of the same amount. The change in the permanent component of income is expected to bring about a decrease in labor force participation. The same change of the transitory component in the opposite direction is expected to stimulate an increase in market activities. The direction of the net outcome depends, therefore, on which income effect is stronger. Indeed, the negative sign of $b_{me\cdot x}$ provides evidence that the effect of transitory income outweighs the permanent income effect![43]

With further computations, elasticity measures of y_t for each of the 12 groups were derived.[44] These had, by my calculations, a weighted mean equal to -0.85. Several other checks supported the finding that the effect of the transitory component of income exceeded the effect of the permanent component of income. Consistent with this finding was the fact that for 11 out of 12 cases, average employment rates for wives whose husbands were unemployed during 1949 were higher than for those whose husbands were fully employed.[45]

The theoretical support for the stronger effect of transitory income is based on two ideas. The first is the permanent income hypothesis that states that families attempt to maintain long-run levels of consumption throughout periods of fluctuating income. The entrance of the wife into the labor force when the husband's income drops is a way of accomplishing this. Indeed, we might think of a "permanent consumption hypothesis" that explains income maintenance.[46] The second is the cross effect of the lowered earnings (or "wage rate") of the husband on the wife's decision to work. In fact, unemployment of the husband (an important cause of negative y_t) will permit him to assume some of the duties of homework.[47] The family decision about the allocation of work among its members will reflect the positive market wage of the wife and the currently zero market wage coupled with some positive home wage of the husband.

[43] *Ibid.*, pp. 81–82.

[44] *Ibid.*, p. 81.

[45] *Ibid.*, p. 79.

[46] This semantic subtlety was suggested to me by Margaret G. Reid.

[47] Hearings before Congress on the problem of depressed areas during the late 1950's are full of not-so-funny examples of a virtual switch in work roles between the long-term unemployed husband and the wife who gets a job. See U.S. Senate, Special Committee on Unemployment Problems, (Hearings), 86th Congress, 2d Session.

It is worth noting that the economic reasons for the large effect of y_t relative to y_p must be sufficiently powerful to overcome a statistical reason for a small effect of y_t. The latter reason is that straightforward errors of measurement, which are usually included in the y_t component have, by definition, a zero effect.

Mincer's finding on the effect of the transitory component of income has important implications for the following three related problems.

(*a*) The negative relation between the work rates of wives and their husbands' reported income will be larger (in absolute value) in short time spans and in cross-sections than over the long run. In cross-sections, families whose husbands' incomes are below the mean will show abnormally high work rates by wives because of the general tendency for these low level incomes to contain negative transitory components. Correspondingly, wives' work rates will be abnormally low among families whose incomes are above the mean. These effects help resolve the contradiction between the apparent, strong negative relation in cross-sections with the apparent positive relation over time.

(*b*) The relatively large effect of y_t supports the contention that wives of unemployed husbands are more likely to enter the labor market. A negative effect operates on the negative value that y_t has when the husband is unemployed, and the result on labor force participation is positive. The "added worker hypothesis" goes further and maintains that general unemployment induces secondary workers (among whom wives are the most numerous) to enter the labor force more than it discourages participation among them (see pp. 62 ff.). Mincer pointed to the elasticity of the wage effect (equal to 1.50) and the elasticity of y_t (equal to −1.42) for the modal group and suggested that the two effects would approximately offset each other during widespread unemployment.[48] If, instead, we use the elasticity for y_t weighted over all groups (equal to −0.85), then the wage effect would seem to win out, and there would be a net diminishment of labor force participation among wives. In chapter 3, I will offer more evidence that this is the case.

(*c*) The observed comparison of labor force participation rates between white and nonwhite married women shows nonwhites with higher rates at given income levels (see Tables 39–41 of Appendix B). We presume that at the same reported income the permanent income of the whites will exceed that of nonwhites so the transitory component will be "more negative" or "less positive" for whites. The stronger effect of y_t, then, would indicate that work rates of white wives should exceed those

[48] *Ibid.*, p. 96.

of nonwhites at similar incomes.[49] Note, however, that any general tendency for nonwhite incomes to contain more errors of measurement than white incomes would operate to show higher nonwhite work rates.[50] But if the y_t components are real and are not offset by errors, then the white-nonwhite differentials to be explained are even larger than the observed differentials. A large part of chapter 3 discusses the differences in work rates by race.

The research of Arnold Katz lends a bit of support to Mincer's hypothesis on the effect of transitory income.[51] Katz studied the labor force behavior of secondary workers in families where the husband was unemployed in 1958. He found that labor force participation increased the longer the head was unemployed and the greater was the decline in income relative to the year preceding. Additional parts of his research, discussed below, do not appear to offer such clear-cut support, however.

Katz divided his sample into three occupational groups based on the unemployment rates (high, medium, low) of the occupations of the husbands.

[49] Let y_c = current income and the subscripts w and n refer to whites and nonwhites, respectively, and assume $y_{cw} = y_{cn}$.

therefore,

$$y_{pw} + y_{tw} = y_{cw} - y_{cn} - y_{pn} + y_{tn} \quad (1)$$

$$(y_{pn} - y_{pw}) = -(y_{tn} - y_{tw}) \quad (2)$$

We assume $y_{pw} > y_{pn}$. Therefore $y_{tw} < y_{tn}$.

Restricting Model II to income variables only and assuming that the income effects are the same for both color groups, we have:

$$m_w = b_p y_{pw} + b_t y_{tw} \quad (3)$$

$$m_n = b_p y_{pn} + b_t y_{tn} \quad (4)$$

$$(4) - (3)\; m_n - m_w = b_p(y_{pn} - y_{pw}) + b_t(y_{tn} - y_{tw}) \quad (5)$$

Given (2), m_n will be less than m_w as long as $|b_t| > |b_p|$.

[50] Add an error component, y_e, to the formulation of the preceding footnote:

$$y_{pw} + y_{tw} + y_{ew} = y_{cw} = y_{cn} = y_{pn} + y_{tn} + y_{en} \quad (1')$$

Clearly it is possible that both $y_{pw} > y_{pn}$ and $y_{tw} > y_{tn}$ if $y_{ew} < y_{en}$ by a sufficient amount. Then,

$$m_n - m_w = b_p(y_{pn} - y_{pw}) + b_t(y_{tn} - y_{tw}) + b_e(y_{en} - y_{ew}) \quad (5')$$

Therefore, on the assumption that $b_e = 0$, the negative effects of b_p and b_t operating on negative quantities $(y_{pn} - y_{pw})$ and $(y_{tn} - y_{tw})$ would yield a positive amount for the difference $m_n - m_w$.

[51] Arnold Katz, "Cyclical Unemployment and the Secondary Family Worker" (unpublished manuscript). Secondary workers in this study comprise 1,241 persons over 14 years of age living in 850 families. Each family included a husband and wife. The husband was not. of course. a secondary worker.

On the assumption that unemployment of a husband is less anticipated if he is in an occupation with low average rates of unemployment, Katz found that participation of secondary workers "increases more when likely family income expectations are disappointed."[52] Mincer suggested that this was especially favorable to his hypothesis, since the y_t effect mainly concerns short-run and unexpected changes in income.[53] The result that Katz reported may also reflect two other considerations: first, the work rates of the wives of husbands who were unemployment-prone and likely to be in low level occupations were probably already high. The rates of these wives would have had less room for increases. Second, husbands who were not so likely to experience unemployment tended to be in the high status occupations. Their wives consequently were likely to have had more education and relatively high earnings abilities that facilitated employment (that is, getting jobs that would "pay" even over a short run for the disruption and effort in entering the labor force).

Katz did not find that illness of the husband (another source of negative y_t) led to any significant change in participation by other family members. Of course, the ability of the unemployed husband to help out around the home is by no means as likely when he is sick; indeed, he may be the cause for more homework by the wife.

In general, this interesting study by Katz testified to the mobility and flexibility of the labor force. More particularly, we can conclude that secondary workers in families where the head becomes unemployed are likely to enter the labor force. We cannot determine from Katz's study, however, which of the two components of income, y_p or y_t, has the stronger influence on the labor supply of the wife. Nor were the more basic predictions about income and substitution (or wage) effects tested, for Katz was interested in the changes in labor supplied and not in the levels.

In two other large-scale studies using survey data, the theoretical predictions of the economic model of labor force participation are put to a test and appear to hold up fairly well. The first study is by Marion B. Sobol, who used the data from the Scripps Population Foundation's survey in 1955 of 2,700 white wives.[54] She employed a multiple regression model to determine the current labor force status of 2,294 wives, aged 18 to 39, who were not currently pregnant. Current labor force status is

[52] *Ibid.*, p. 8.

[53] Mincer, "Labor Force Participation of Married Women," p. 96, footnote 43.

[54] Marion B. Sobol, "Correlates of Present and Future Work Status of Married Women" (Unpublished Ph.D. dissertation, University of Michigan, 1960). See her paper, "Commitment to Work," in Nye and Hoffman, *The Employed Mother in America*, pp. 40–63.

measured in the form of a dummy (or dichotomous) variable that takes the value 1 if the wife is in the labor force or 0 if the wife is not in the labor force. Table 4 shows her main results. We might consider the variables, income of the husband and education of the wife, as proxies for Y and W, respectively.

Since I use this same body of data and report my results in chapter 3, only a few comments will be made here.

TABLE 4

REGRESSION RESULTS OF THE STUDY BY SOBOL

CURRENT LABOR FORCE STATUS OF WIVES[a]

Independent Variable	Units of Measure	Regression Coefficients (1) Arithmetic[b]	Regression Coefficients (2) Standardized[c]
Husband's income....	Assigned Value: 0, 1, 2, ..., 9; Dollars: 0, 1–999, 1,000–1,999, ..., 8,000 or more	−.0028	−.0125 (.0020)
Wife's education..	Assigned Value: 0 (8 grades or less), 1 (Some or all High School), 2 (College)	.0045	.0056 (.0020)
Worked prior to marriage	Dummy (1 if yes)	.0070	.0066 (.0020)
Children under 6......	Dummy (1 if yes)	−.0332	−.0368 (.0019)
Children over 6.........	Dummy (1 if yes)	−.0057	−.0065 (.0024)
Expects more children...	Dummy (1 if yes)	−.0016	−.0019[d] (.0021)
Married more than once..	Dummy (1 if yes)	.0015	.0010[d] (.0019)
Year married.	Last 2 digits of year married (thus, younger wives will tend to have a larger number here)	.0033	.0041[d] (.0028)

Source: Marion B. Gross Sobol, "Correlates of Present and Future Work Status of Married Women," (Unpublished Ph.D. dissertation, University of Michigan, 1960), p. 32.

[a] Dependent variable, labor force status: 1 if in the labor force, 0 if not in the labor force. The sample size was 2,294. The multiple correlation, or R^2, was .16.

[b] No standard errors were reported for arithmetic coefficients.

[c] These are beta coefficients of normalized equations wherein each variable is divided by its standard deviation. Numbers in parentheses are the standard errors of the coefficients.

[d] Coefficients are *not* significant by the criterion of a t-value less than 1.96.

(*a*) The economic variables are significant and possess the predicted signs. They contribute relatively little to the explained variation in labor force participation, however; most is due to the variable indicating the presence of children under 6 years of age. By itself this variable accounts for 12 per cent of the variation according to the matrix of simple correlations Sobol presents, and all the variables together explain only 16 per cent of the variation. That the presence of preschool age children would be an important determinant of labor force behavior among wives in a cross-section needs no explanation. I should note that a relatively low multiple correlation is common among cross-section regressions with disaggregated data.

(*b*) It is interesting to check on the relative magnitudes of the income and wage (here, education) effects. By assigning "potential earnings" to the wife based on her educational status, we note that each unit of education would contribute about $600 of additional earnings.[55] A unit of education, therefore, equals roughly 6/10 of the $1,000-unit that measures the husband's income in the regression. It turns out that by using the arithmetic coefficients, the "wage rate effect" just about equals the income effect in absolute value.[56]

(*c*) From the standpoint of examining long-run forces affecting labor force participation, the statistical significance of the variable, "worked prior to marriage," appears to me to have little economic significance. If we are to explain the wife's current work on the basis of her having worked previously, the obvious question is: why did she work before? Surely, one explanation is that she could earn a high wage. Since this factor would also determine her current labor force status, the presence of the variable for "prior work" may rob the wage proxy of some of its effect.

(*d*) It is difficult to interpret "year married" except as a proxy for either the age of the wife or for how late in life the wife (of a given age) married. The positive sign tells us that younger wives are more likely to be working or that wives of a given age who married late are more likely to be working. One explanation for higher work rates of young wives is that their husbands, who also tend to be young, are earning incomes below their expected lifetime average level. As a result of this life-cycle pattern their incomes have, in effect, a negative component—a type of

[55] The median income of females who worked full-time in 1957 was approximately $2,400, $3,000, and $3,600 for the three educational groups used by Sobol. (See *Current Population Reports,* P-50, No. 27, p. 37.)

[56] The units of the education variable measure about $600 wage-equivalent units and have an arithmetic regression coefficient of .0045; the income units are approximately in $1,000 units and have a coefficient of −.0028. Note that $600 \times .0045 \approx 1000 \times .0028$. See pp. 92 ff. for an elaboration of this technique with these data.

negative y_t. On the basis of Mincer's study, we expect the negative y_t to have a positive effect; in other words, the wife is likely to work to make up the temporary income deficiency. In the case of wives who married at relatively older ages, a greater likelihood of working may be attributable in part to their having already established something of a career by the time they married.

(*e*) The variables for remarriage, age, and several other characteristics are discussed further in chapter 3.

The second of the two large studies was conducted by James N. Morgan and others[57] and was based on a sample of 1,828 white and 231 nonwhite wives. Two dependent variables were used: the first is the same dichotomous variable (0–1) for current labor force status; the second is a longer run concept, "years worked while married." Summaries of the results are shown in Tables 5 and 6. The independent variables listed were included in the multiple regression in the form of a group of dummy variables. Thus, there is no single coefficient of the variable; rather, separate coefficients for each member of the group. The signs entered in these tables in the middle columns reveal the general influence of the group of dummy variables, and where two variables are combined the separate effect of each is noted. The first two lines in Table 5 each show interaction effects for two combined characteristics. The interaction of race (N = nonwhite) and age of children, for example, revealed that the negative effect of young children was weaker when the wife was nonwhite. The columns giving the beta coefficients and *F*-ratios indicate the statistical significance of the variables in terms of their contribution to the explained variation of labor force participation.

Unlike Sobol's data, this sample contains wives of all ages and both races. Consequently there is a rather wide range of variation that can be explained (in a statistical sense) by these two variables, and this is borne out by their high *F*-values, shown in both Tables 5 and 6. The positive effect of the education of the wife and the negative effect of income are again demonstrated in Table 5. Three other results shown in Table 5 "agree" with the theoretical expectations based on the model of this study.

(*a*) "City size" and "extent of state unemployment" reveal wage rate effects in the sense that wages (or employment opportunities) are less in small towns and rural areas and less when unemployment is high.

(*b*) The "difference in education of heads and wives" may be interpreted in terms of a cross-substitution effect. For example, an advanced

[57] James N. Morgan, Martin H. David, Wilbur J. Cohen, and Harvey E. Brazier, *Income and Welfare in the United States* (New York: McGraw-Hill, 1962), pp. 107–39.

education of a wife would indicate a high earnings capacity—high relative to the husband's earnings ability as indicated by his low education. Thus, the wife in this example would engage in relatively more market work on the basis of the family's allocation of time to market work, homework and leisure between husband and wife. The authors give a different explanation that is more sociological: "the wife sets the living standards for the

TABLE 5

REGRESSION RESULTS OF THE STUDY OF MORGAN *et al.*

CURRENT LABOR FORCE STATUS OF WIVES

CHARACTERISTICS USED TO EXPLAIN LABOR FORCE PARTICIPATION IN 1959 (FOR SPENDING UNIT WIVES)

Characteristics of Spending Unit Wives	Relative Importance (Beta Coefficients)	Sign of Effect	Significance (*F*-Ratios)
Age (A_w) and education (E) of wife	.287	$(A_w)^a-$ $(E)^b+$	19.81[g]
Race of wife (N=nonwhite) and age of children (A_c)	.281	$(N)^c+$ $(A_c)^d+$	38.09[g]
Attitude of heads toward wives working	.162	+	9.04[g]
Gross factor income of heads and wives, excluding wives' earnings	.157	−	6.61[g]
Plan to help parents or children	.080	+	5.15[g]
Population of cities	.078	+	2.94[h]
Extent of unemployment in states	.071	−	3.04[h]
Difference in education of wives and heads	.065	$(W\text{-}H)^e-$	2.04
Physical condition	.063	$(Dis)^f-$	3.19[h]
Frequency of unemployment of heads	.063	0	1.37

Source: James N. Morgan, Martin H. David, Wilbur J. Cohen, and Harvey E. Brazier, *Income and Welfare in the United States* (New York: McGraw-Hill, 1962), pp. 109 ff.

Note: No R^2 was given.

[a] (A_w) −The older the wife, the less likely she is working

[b] (E) +The greater the education of the wife, the more likely she is working

[c] (N) +Nonwhite wives are more likely to be working

[d] (A_c) +The older the children the more likely the wife is working

[e] $(W\text{-}H)$ +The more the wife's education exceeds the husband's, the more likely she is working

[f] (Dis) −The poorer the physical condition of the wife the less likely she is working

[g] Significant at probability level of .01

[h] Significant at probability level of .05

family, and the husband's ability to meet them without the wife working usually depends on the relation of his education to hers."[58] Two of the results in Table 5 are difficult to discuss with the model at hand.

(*c*) The variable measuring the "attitude of the head" does operate as we would expect: a family decision for the wife to work tends to be made when an important member of the family, the husband, is favorably in-

[58] *Ibid.*, p. 116.

clined toward the decision. It is difficult for an economist to go beyond this lame interpretation. Perhaps it reveals a rationalization process—given the decision to work, the individuals concerned express favorable attitudes toward working. Or it might be that both work by the wife and a favorable attitude reflect the ability of the wife to get a "good job."

(*d*) The variable, "plans to help parents," is in the category of explanations based on what the wife will do with her earnings.[59] It seems to be rather arbitrary, however, which bundle of goods and servcies one would choose to ask about in this connection. Why not ask if the wife works to buy a new car, or help pay for the house, or buy a new dress, and so on?

(*e*) The variable indicating the husband's "frequency of unemployment" shows no effect. Comparisons with other studies are difficult because the concepts differ.[60] Both Katz and Mincer found that unemployment of the husband, measured as "weeks or months not worked," had a positive effect on work by the wife. In chapter 3 I report a positive effect when the husband is "currently unemployed" that is significant in the 1-in-1,000 sample, although insignificant in the sample from the Growth of American Families study.

Table 6 shows the results of the regression when the dependent variable is a measure of labor supply that applies to the entire period of the woman's marriage. Two comments will be made here that refer to the further work I do with this type of data in chapter 3. First, "years worked while married" obviously will tend to be positively associated with years married. In using similar data, I measure this interesting lifetime supply-of-labor concept as a ratio, years worked over years married. This avoids the mechanical relation between age and years worked. A second point concerns the very puzzling negative sign of the education variable. To the extent that education serves as a proxy for the wage available to the wife, its negative sign (when other factors are held constant) represents a failure of the model's prediction. I give special attention to this problem in chapter 3, and I believe the puzzle is largely resolved.

A study by Richard Rosett of 1,592 households from the Survey of

[59] Stanley Lebergott, for example, suggests that today's wife works to buy a car or a new appliance. Lebergott, *op. cit.*, p. 401.

[60] The dependent variable in the regression of Morgan *et al.* is the current labor force status of the wife. The unemployment variable in the regression refers to the past unemployment experience of the husband measured by the following categories: "frequent unemployment," "occasional unemployment," "short spells only," "infrequent," "never," "entered the labor force recently," "not ascertained," and "self-employed." Relying as they do on the memory and judgment of the person interviewed, these categories may be too imprecise. Moreover, there is no clear reason why past unemployment would be strongly related to the current labor force status of the wife.

Consumer Finances is interesting for the addition of variables on the financial position of the family—debt, property income, and liquid assets.[61] Mincer has suggested that large asset holdings and the absence of contractual obligations would give families a source of funds when income fell that would be an alternative to work by the wife.[62] On this issue the results from Rosett's study are inconclusive. Liquid assets did not significantly affect the labor supply of the wife. Property income had a significant negative effect, and it is highly correlated with liquid assets. Also, the two variables are positively correlated with permanent income, a fact that adds to the difficulty of interpreting the findings.

TABLE 6

REGRESSION RESULTS OF THE STUDY OF MORGAN *et al.*
YEARS WORKED DURING MARRIAGE

CHARACTERISTICS USED TO EXPLAIN THE NUMBER OF YEARS WORKED (FOR SPENDING UNIT WIVES)

Characteristics of Spending Unit Wives	Relative Importance (Beta Coefficients)	Sign of Effect	Significance (*F*-Ratios)
Age	.367	+	55.15[b]
Number of living children of the head	.238	−	34.79[b]
Attitude of heads toward wives working	.128	+	5.75[b]
Race	.112	(*N*)[a]+	30.82[b]
Education	.091	−	2.54[b]
Physical condition	.068	(*Dis*)[a]−	3.79[b]

Source: Morgan *et al.*, *op. cit.*, pp. 118 ff.
$R^2 = .19$
[a] See the notes to Table 5 for an explanation of the symbols, (*N*) and (*Dis*).
[b] Significant at probability level of .01.

There were two serious defects in the data used by Rosett. First, neither the amount of work nor the wage of the wife was known, only her income for the year. The dependent variable used was the ratio of wife's income to husband's income. Second, the only clue to her education was the educational attainment of her husband. Any attempt to analyze Rosett's findings involves too much speculation about how his variables are related to those specified in the model used in this book.

The final two studies are smaller in scale and are of less relevance to

[61] Richard Rosett, "Working Wives: An Econometric Study," in *Studies in Household Economic Behavior*, ed. Thomas F. Dernberg *et al.* (New Haven: Yale University Press, 1958) pp. 51–100.

[62] Mincer, "Labor Force Participation of Married Women," especially p. 75.

this study. Thomas A. Mahoney[63] and John Korbel[64] both used the prior work experience of the wife as a variable and found this to be the most important factor. The weakness of this variable, from my standpoint, has already been discussed[65] (see item [*c*] in the discussion of Sobol's research, p. 34). Mahoney also included an attitudinal variable, "the wife's attitude toward work," that was determined and scaled by inter-

TABLE 7

RELATION OF STEADINESS OF FAMILY INCOME PRIOR TO 1954 AND WIFE'S LABOR FORCE PARTICIPATION FROM 1954 TO 1956

WIFE'S WORK STATUS 1954–56[a]	HISTORY OF FAMILY INCOME PRIOR TO 1954				
	All	Rising	Steady	Falling	Fluctuating
1. Not working	67%	67%	73%	58%	64%
2. Working	18	20	16	15	25
3. Started working	7	7	6	19	5
4. Stopped working	3	4	3	2	2
5. Started-and-stopped or stopped-and-started	3	2	2	6	4
Number of cases	879	272	432	53	122

Source: Ford Re-interview Study: Q: "Has your family income been quite steady during the past few years, or has it been going up, or going down, or changed from time to time?" Sobol, "Correlates of Present and Future Work Status of Married Women," p. 42.

[a] These categories are mutually exclusive. Thus, "wife not working" refers to women who never worked throughout the period 1954–56. Similarly, "wife started working" refers to women who started working at some time during 1954–56, and have continued working from that time until the time of the last interview (1956).

viewers, and this variable was also important statistically. It seems likely, however, that circularity is involved in this relation. The wife who works says she favors working; the wife who does not work says she favors not

[63] Thomas A. Mahoney, "Factors Determining the Labor Force Participation of Married Women," *Industrial and Labor Relations Review* (July, 1961) pp. 563–77. The sample used consisted of 450 wives in St. Paul, Minnesota.

[64] John Korbel, "Female Labor Force Mobility and Its Simulations," *The Economics of Human Resources*, ed. Mark Perlman (Baltimore: The Johns Hopkins Press, 1963) pp. 55–73. This sample consisted of 574 women in Wisconsin. The study is an outgrowth of the work begun by Guy Orcutt, Martin Greenberg, Alice Rivlin, and John Korbel, *Microanalysis of Socioeconomic Systems* (New York: Harper & Brothers, 1961), chaps. ix–xi, pp. 161–231. In these chapters work by wives was related solely to demographic factors.

[65] The goal of Korbel and Orcutt, on the other hand, is to predict labor force participation of wives in the short run, often as an intermediate step in analyzing a different problem. Previous work experience is unquestionably an excellent variable for this purpose.

working. Like the attitudinal variables in the study by Morgan *et al.*, this finding is difficult to interpret.

Disaggregated Time Series

Panel surveys, wherein observations on the same individuals are recorded at different points in time, are rare in economics. One set of panel data, referred to by Sobol,[66] related the change in family income to the wife's labor force participation over a 3-year period. The ordinary income–labor force relation is placed in a dynamic context as is shown in Table 7.

Two percentages in particular stand out: (*a*) 19 per cent of the wives whose family incomes had been falling started working (row 3), and (*b*) 25 per cent of wives whose family incomes fluctuated worked continually over the 3-year period (row 2). These figures are significantly larger than those in the other columns of rows 3 and 2. The first is a striking confirmation of Mincer's hypothesis that a decline in a family's income leads the wife to enter the labor force. The second implies that income instability, per se, is associated with relatively more work by wives. Although control over such factors as age and presence of children would be helpful, Table 7 illustrates the fruitfulness of tracing the effects of economic changes over time without the blurring that goes on in aggregation.

Summary

This chapter has discussed and illustrated methods and materials for empirical research of the labor force participation of married women. It is clear that cross-section data have provided the richest source for statistical research. My empirical work, which is presented in the next chapter, also deals mostly with this type of data. The models for cross-section data that have been discussed in this chapter are cast in the statistical form of regression analysis. The theory underlying the regression model is, basically, price theory.

Economic theory has suggested certain expected effects of several variables: income, wages, the presence of children, and so forth. The review of previous studies offered a first check on how well these expectations were fulfilled. General agreement with the theory was the rule, although this judgment anticipates the reconciliation I make later (p. 98) with the one important exception—the instance when a "wage" variable (education) had a negative effect on the labor supply of married women (see p. 37).

[66] Sobol, "Correlates of Present and Future Work Status of Married Women."

Three general types of variables have been discussed: economic, demographic, and "tastes." Demographic variables have the most explanatory power when the units of observation are individual wives rather than averages of groups of wives. This is neither surprising nor necessarily indicative of any great importance of demographic effects in a different context, such as a time series. For example, the finding that wives over 60 years of age and wives with young children are not likely to be working would not be particularly important for explaining secular trends unless the age composition and fertility rates have changed markedly. As we have seen, however, the demographic changes that have occurred over time have not been large and have certainly not operated in a single direction in their effect on work by wives.

The economist sometimes looks upon demographic variables as proxies for tastes. In connection with work by women, however, tastes more commonly refer to social factors, generally subsumed under the rubric, "changing social attitudes." A major difficulty here is to devise variables capable of quantification that will "measure" tastes in some acceptable fashion. Unless one is interested in this variable for its own sake, it is no alternative to consider "social attitudes" as a residual variable. My relegation of the discussion of tastes to an appendix does not imply a denial of the importance of the variable. Instead and more modestly, I pose the question: to what extent can the variation in labor force participation rates of married women be explained by an economic model that does not explicitly include the tastes variable? I do suggest that economic forces may be more causally important than surface appearances imply, and that changes in social attitudes are sometimes attributable to and only reflect the other forces.

A brief digression will illustrate this point. Consider the large rise in the labor force participation of women, including married women, during World War II. A substantial increase in the demand for labor occurred simultaneously with a contraction in the (customary) male labor force, and the wage rates for women thereby rose sharply. The income of families fell wherever the husband (or working son) was drafted, and the same act reduced the demand for the services of homework of the wife or mother—immediately and, with a decline in births, over the span of several years. The income fall was plainly of a transitory nature, and the level of family expenditures may have been maintained over this period with the entrance of the wife into the labor force. Insofar as special (tangible) inducements were made for working women in this period, these were services complementary to work participation; on the other hand, amusement taxes and enforced curtailment of recreational activities acted as a "tax" on one type of leisure (and a "subsidy" to work). With all this going on it may well be that the dependent variable, labor force participation of married women during World War II, would be largely explained with only a limited appeal to "changing social attitudes" or credit to "patriotism" nudging the supply curve to the right.

This is not to say that World War II had no impact on the trend of rising work rates of wives, for once the war had set in motion the extraordinary events described above, these effects were bound to extend past

TABLE 8

LABOR FORCE PARTICIPATION RATES OF MARRIED WOMEN, HUSBAND PRESENT, AGED 20–34, AND BIRTH RATES OF WOMEN EVER MARRIED, AGED 20–34, FOR SELECTED YEARS

Labor Force Participation Rate (Per Cent)[a]	Year	Comment with Regard to the Year	Birth Rate[b]
19	1940	Prior to the war	1.52
25	1950	When all of the wives aged 20-34 were eligible to be in the labor force during some part of World War II	1.64
28	1960	When only the wives aged 30 and older would have had any labor force experience during World War II	2.17
32	1964	When none of the wives aged 20-34 were of labor force age (i.e. 14 or older) during World War II	2.30

[a] Labor force participation rates for 1940, 1950, and 1960 are from U.S. Department of Labor, Bureau of Labor Statistics, "Special Labor Force Report, No. 13," Reprint No. 2364, p. 3, and the figure for 1964 was derived from "Special Labor Force Report, No. 50," Reprint No. 2457, p. A-8.

[b] The number of children ever born per 1,000 women ever married by age and marital status for the noninstitutional population of the United States is given in Current Population Reports, "Population Characteristics," Series P-20, No. 136, April 16, 1965, p. 2. For the number of married women by age in 1940 and 1950, the source is No. 108, July 12, 1961, p. 18 of the same series. The number of married women by age in 1960 and 1964 is found in No. 135, April 28, 1965, pp. 9–10 of the same series.

the duration of the war itself. Undoubtedly, attitudes more favorable to work by females were inculcated. Further, the investments made by women in acquiring job skills and in the adjustments to working as a way of life were investments that could be drawn upon in the future years, either by continuing to work after the war or by returning to work after a period of withdrawal from the labor force.

These effects are vividly noticeable in the European nations where the heavy casualties of World War II among the male population reinforced the trend of high work rates among the cohort of adult women during the war. In Europe, moreover, the postwar manpower shortage was partly responsible for increased work rates of females (wives included) who reached working age after the end of the war. In the United States, on the other hand, the persistence of high and increasing work rates after the war among wives who were too young to be in the war-time labor force is evidence of the strength of the longer run economic forces, particularly when we take into account the rise in birth rates during the postwar period. This point is supported by Table 8.

Of course, the Korean conflict during 1950–53 was an intervening event, but this did not entail a major mobilization. I would suggest that the above figures indicate that the impact of World War II should not be exaggerated. Unless one was prepared to argue that the effects of the war on attitudes and institutions remained significant 20 years after its end, the rise in work rates of wives would appear to be evidence of longer run forces.

III

A Presentation of Empirical Work

The Plan of the Chapter and a Preview of the White-Nonwhite Differential

THE EMPIRICAL work of this chapter consists primarily of multiple regressions with cross-section data. In the first section the regression model for aggregative data is applied to several samples of observations on cities and standard metropolitan areas from the 1940, 1950, and 1960 censuses. In the last section of this chapter, two sets of survey data are examined—the Growth of American Families Survey and the 1-in-1,000 Sample. Regression techniques are again the principal tool of analysis. This section has three objectives: to exploit the larger number of variables and observations these bodies of data provide; to check on the results of the aggregative models; and to test suggested explanations for the differences in work rates by white and nonwhite wives. The application of the basic model to data on nonwhites and the attempt to explain the labor force behavior of nonwhite wives receive major emphasis throughout this chapter.

Two differences between labor force participation behavior of white and nonwhite wives stand out in the published statistics and call for an explanation. First, nonwhite wives have higher labor force participation rates at a given moment in time. Second, nonwhite wives have shown a slower rate of increase in participation over time. Table 9 brings out the first point.

The effects of the two principal economic factors, husbands' and wives' earnings, will not explain the higher rates for nonwhite wives. Since the wage for white wives is higher, this factor exacerbates the problem; that is, we would expect lower work rates for nonwhite wives on this account. On the other hand, if we allow for the husband's income, the difference by color narrows, but it still remains substantial. This is shown in the last part of Table 9 (compare the rates for the two income classes with the total), and more evidence is presented in Appendix B (Tables 39, 40, and 41).

The second difference in labor force behavior between white and nonwhite wives is shown by the time series data in Table 10. First, note that the work rates of females show an upward trend for whites and a decline or flat trend for nonwhites. The trend over time is positive for wives of both colors, however; the difference to be explained here is the much slower rate of increase on the part of nonwhite wives. We might surmise, parenthetically, that the sharp decrease in work rates of nonwhite single women largely reflects two trends: (1) the gains in precollege school attendance that have been especially pronounced among nonwhites during the past twenty years, and (2) the negative effect on work of elderly nonwhite females, stemming from increases in income and from welfare

TABLE 9

THE PER CENT OF MARRIED WOMEN, HUSBAND PRESENT, IN THE LABOR FORCE, BY COLOR AND SELECTED CHARACTERISTICS, MARCH, 1961

	White	Nonwhite
By residence[a]		
Total	31.6	45.0
Urban	31.9	47.7
Rural Nonfarm	31.4	41.7
Rural Farm	30.7	32.1
By presence and age of children[a]		
None under 18 years of age	36.0	51.0
6–17 years of age	40.6	58.2
Some under 6 years of age	18.6	31.9
By income of husband, year preceding (selected categories),[b] March for 1959, 1960, 1961[c]		
Total	30.4	44.3
$2,000–$2,999	33.8	43.1
$3,000–$3,999	36.0	44.6

[a] Source: U.S. Department of Labor, Bureau of Labor Statistics, "Special Labor Force Report, No. 20," p. 9.

[b] The two income categories have the largest number of observations for nonwhites among six categories.

[c] The observations for three years were pooled to increase the sample size. See Table 10 in Appendix B for the full listing of data and the source.

legislation that have probably had a relatively greater impact on this group. Both trends have slowed down (in relative terms, nonwhite to white) during the past few years and, as is implicit in Table 10, so has the relative decline in work rates of nonwhite single women.

A final point is that marriage rates are higher for white females. Thus, the secular increase in work rates among married women has a larger effect on the total female work rates for whites. This point may also have a slight bearing on the cross-section differences shown in Table 9. If marriage selects favorably among women with regard to education, intelligence, and so forth, then the higher marriage rates among white women may indicate a less favorable selectivity at the margin. On these grounds the work rates of white wives would be less since educational attainment and intelligence imply a high earnings ability and high work rates. This line of reasoning assumes that nonwhite females who marry are similarly more intelligent and more educated than those who do not marry.

Regression Results for the Cross-Section Aggregated Data from the Census

The application of a regression model to cross-section aggregates was extensively discussed in chapter 2. The theoretical model that was stated on page 10 relates work by married women (M) to: income from non-labor sources (Y_n), husband's earnings (Y), the wife's wage (W), children (C), and tastes (T).

TABLE 10

Labor Force Participation Rates of Women by Marital Status and Color for Selected Years

	Wives, Husband Present			Total Female	
	Year	White	Nonwhite	White	Nonwhite
Census data[a]	1930	not available	not available	21.8	40.4
	1940	12.5	27.3	24.5	37.3
	1950	20.7	31.8	28.4	37.1
Current population reports[b]	1950	22.8	37.0	30.5	41.1
	1957	28.7	40.2	34.7	45.5
	1960	30.0	41.0	35.5	46.3
	1964[c]	33.4	45.4	35.8	42.9

[a] Source: Stanley Lebergott, "Population Change and the Supply of Labor," in *Demographic and Economic Change in Developed Countries*, National Bureau of Economic Research (Princeton: Princeton University Press, 1958), p. 389; and Gertrude Bancroft, *The American Labor Force* (New York: John Wiley and Sons, 1958), p. 31.

[b] Series P-50 of the Bureau of Census.

[c] Special Labor Force Report, No. 50, *op. cit.*, p. A-9, Table C.

$$\text{Model I: } M = a_1Y_n + b_1Y + b_2W + a_4C + a_5T + V$$

For use with the census data for cross-section aggregates, we looked at Mincer's study (pages 22–24), and the regression equation similar to the following form:

$$m = a_1y_n + b_1y + b_2w + a_4c + \ldots + v$$

The observations for the regressions of this section were gathered from the cities (1940), standard metropolitan areas (1950), and standard statistical metropolitan areas (1960) that had a population of 250,000 or more. The latter two areas are referred to as SMA's. The regression results for all three census years are contained in Tables 11–22. A listing of symbols and definitions for the variables used in the tables is given in Appendix A, pages 123–27, along with the sources, means, and standard deviations of the variables.

The form of the regression in the tables is given in the second column, where *A* stands for arithmetic form and *L* for logarithmic (to the base 10) form. The logarithmic regressions are based on a model that is multiplicative in the relation of the independent variables to the dependent variable. To illustrate:

$$m = a_o y_n^{a'_1} y^{b'_1} w^{b'_2} \ldots v$$

where a logarithmic transformation would yield:

$$\log m = \log a_0 + a'_1 \log y_n + b'_1 \log y + b'_2 \log w + \ldots$$

and the coefficients, a'_1, b'_1, b'_2, and so on are equivalent to elasticities. If any variable in a regression is ever zero or negative, then the arithmetic value of this variable is used in the logarithmic regression. The standard errors of the regression coefficients will always be in parentheses.

It is convenient to begin with the 1950 census data. Mincer's study of area aggregations, discussed at length in chapter 2, applied to 1950, and most of my experimentation with various functional forms of regressions and selections of different variables was with these data. The first table of regression results (Table 11) will be examined in some detail, and with this examination behind us the remaining tables will be discussed more briefly.

Regression Results with Total Married Women with the 1950 Census Data: Main Results (Table 11)

The northern regional regression that Mincer presented adapts easily to a nationwide base when a dummy variable to account for the difference in levels by regions (designated by r) is included in the model. Regressions on lines 5 and 6 in Table 11 show that the coefficients of the variables for income (y) and wages (w) are similar to those in Mincer's regressions, which are reproduced in lines 9–10. The coefficients of the variables for the effects of children and unemployment are significant, however, and this differs from Mincer's results. I have suggested that this difference stems from minor computational errors by Mincer. (See my regressions with the northern data on lines 7–8, also reproduced from Table 3.)

The first two lines of Table 11 differ from the Mincer model in the addition of the variable, y_n, which represents non-labor income—income other than wages, salaries, or earnings from self-employment. The measure of this variable is the median income of this type received per person over 14 years of age in the SMA.

TABLE 11

REGRESSION RESULTS WITH TOTAL MARRIED WOMEN, SMA'S IN 1950[a]

	Line	Form[b]	R^2	Independent Variables									
				Constant	y	w	y_n	r	c	c'	u	e	e'
Total United States, 77 SMA's	1	A	.64	37.94	−.43 (.22)	1.04 (.25)	−.50 (.27)	3.41 (.91)	−.48 (.10)	....	−.40 (.20)	.73 (.37)	....
	2	L	.64	2.75	−.55 (.31)	1.01 (.23)	−.09 (.06)	.16 (.04)	−1.22 (.25)	....	−.10 (.05)	.28 (.19)	....
	3	A	.60	36.55	−.44 (.22)	1.18 (.25)	....	3.55 (.91)	−.43 (.09)	....	−.41 (.21)	....	....
	4	L	.62	2.71	−.59 (.30)	1.15 (.22)	....	.07 (.02)	−1.11 (.24)	....	−.10 (.04)	....	....
	5	A	.55	21.36	−.53 (.24)	1.21 (.27)	....	3.57 (.99)	....	−.31 (.12)	−.55 (.22)	.56 (.40)	....
	6	A	.45	4.74	−.16 (.23)	1.09 (.27)	....	5.16 (.91)	....	....	....	....	....
North only, 57 SMA's	7	A	.56	......	−.84 (.31)	1.48 (.35)	....	....	....	−.53 (.16)	−.56 (.26)	.95 (.45)	....
	8	A	.38	......	−.30 (.29)	1.29 (.31)	....	....	....	....	....	....	....
	9[c]	A	.62	......	−.62 (.21)	1.33 (.11)	....	....	....	−.24 (.61)	−.41 (.53)	....	.12 (.27)
	10[c]	A	.51	......	−.53	1.52	....	....	....	....	....	....	....

[a] Dependent variable: labor force participation rate of married women, husband present.

[b] A = arithmetic; L = logarithmic.

[c] Mincer's regressions (see Table 3, p. 23).

Definitions of independent variables (see Appendix A for sources, means, and standard deviations)

- y median income for male family heads, spouse present, 1949 (hundreds of dollars)
- w median income of females who worked 50–52 weeks in 1949 (hundreds of dollars)
- y_n referred to as non-labor income (hundreds of dollars). See Appendix A for full definition.
- r dummy variable for region: 1 is a southern SMA, 0 otherwise
- c per cent of husband-wife families with one or more children under 18 years of age
- c' per cent of husband-wife families with one or more children under 6 years of age
- u male unemployment rate (in per cent)
- e median years of schooling completed by females, 25 years and older
- e' per cent of the population aged 25 years and older with a completed high school education

We can use these first two lines to indicate how the table is to be read. In line 1 the form of the regression is arithmetic. The multiple correlation is .64. The constant or intercept term is 37.94.[1] The regression coefficient in the next column indicates that for each $100 increase in the income of the husband, the labor force participation rate of married women declines by .43 percentage points.[2] The coefficient of the next variable, income from non-labor sources, just misses statistical significance. (Its *t*-statistic is 1.88.) Given this qualification, however, the coefficient implies that for each $100 increase in non-labor income the labor force participation rate of wives decreases by one-half of a percentage point. Next, we see that for each $100 increase in full-time earnings of females the rate increases by about 1 percentage point. The labor force participation rate of wives in southern SMA's are higher by 3.4 percentage points. The rates decrease by about .5 percentage points for each percentage point increase in families with one or more children under 18, and the rates decline by .4 percentage points for each percentage point increase in male unemployment rates of the SMA. Finally, the rate increases by .7 of a percentage point for each additional year of school completed by females over 25 years of age in the SMA.

In line 2 all the variables except the dummy variable for region are measured in log form, and their coefficients may be looked upon as elasticity measures. The elasticity of husband's income is −.55 and of non-labor income, −.09 (although again the latter variable is not significantly different from zero). Thus, for each 1.0 per cent rise in husband's income we expect a 0.55 per cent decrease in work rates of wives, and for each 1.0 per cent rise in non-labor income about a .1 of a per cent decrease. The wage elasticity (which includes a positive substitution effect and a negative income effect) is positive and about equal to one. These results are all compatible with the arithmetic results. This is brought out in Table 12 which attempts to provide another aid in understanding the regression results.

These results can give us at least a rough estimate of income and sub-

[1] The mean value of labor force participation rates among the 77 SMA's is 22.90. See Table 37 in Appendix A where the means and standard deviations of all the variables used are listed. This will enable the reader to get some idea of the range of values over which the regressions were fitted.

[2] The given point estimates of the regression coefficients will be referred to throughout this study. The rough-and-ready 95 per cent confidence interval of these estimates can be obtained by doubling the value of the standard error (in parentheses) and adding and subtracting this from the coefficient. Whenever the estimate is not statistically significant at the 95 per cent level (in which case the ratio of the coefficient to its standard error, the *t*-statistic, is less than 1.96), this will be brought to the reader's attention.

stitution effects (in elasticity terms). The value of the wage elasticity, unity, may be considered a lower boundary of the pure substitution elasticity. Higher estimates are given by applying formulas (4) and (5) on pages 12–13.

$$a'_3 = b'_2 - a'_1 \left(\frac{W\hat{M}}{Y_n}\right) \qquad (4)$$

$$a'_3 = b'_2 - b'_1 \left(\frac{W\hat{M}}{Y\hat{Q}}\right) \quad \text{where we have assumed } a'_2 = 0 \qquad (5)$$

TABLE 12

"TYPICAL" EFFECTS OF INCOME AND EARNINGS VARIABLES ON THE LABOR FORCE PARTICIPATION RATES OF WIVES USING THE RESULTS OF THE ARITHMETIC AND LOGARITHMIC REGRESSIONS FOR 1950

(LINES 1 AND 2 OF TABLE 11)

VARIABLE	1950 AVERAGE (APPROX.)	HYPOTHETICAL INCREASES OF 10%	COEFFICIENTS		THE USE OF ARITHMETIC AND LOGARITHMIC COEFFICIENTS FOR PREDICTED NEW RATE FROM A BASE LFPR OF 23% TO:	
			Arith.	Log	Arith.	Log
Husband's income, y..	\$3,100	\$310	−0.43	−0.55	21.67%	21.73%
Non-labor income, y_n.	650	65	−0.50	−0.09	22.67	22.79
Wife's full-time earnings, w....	2,000	200	1.04	1.01	25.00	25.30

Source: Table 11 for regression coefficients, lines 1 and 2. Table 37 for mean values of the variables in 1950 for 77 SMA's with populations of 250,000 or more.

Recall that a'_3 is the elasticity of the pure substitution effect of the wife's wage on her labor supply; a'_2 (assumed in [5] to be zero) is the cross-elasticity of the husband's wage on the wife's labor supply; b'_1 and b'_2 are the observed elasticity coefficients of y and w; and the ratios of wife's earnings to non-labor income and of wife's earnings to husband's earnings are the terms of parentheses. (W and Y are the original symbols for wage rates, and w and y are measures of actual earnings, so $W\hat{M} = w$ and $Y\hat{Q} = y$.) The values of the ratios are approximately 3.1 ($=w/y_n$) and .65 ($=w/y$), using the data for the 77 SMA's in 1950 shown in Table 12 or Table 37. The income elasticity (of non-labor income) is a'_1.

Inserting these values into the equations gives us:

$$a_3' = 1.01 - (-.09)(3.1) = 1.29 \qquad (4)$$

and

$$a_3' = 1.01 - (-.55)(.65) = 1.37 \qquad (5)$$

Now let us consider a source of bias in the estimates of the income elasticity term that is due to variations across SMA's in the ratios of the average earnings of wives to the average income from non-labor sources or from husbands.[3] The wife's earnings and the other sources of income are positively related among the SMA's, and the relation is such that relative increases in w are about proportional to relative increases in y, but less than proportional to relative increases in y_n. When the logarithm of w is regressed on the logarithm of y, the coefficient is 1.03. The coefficient so close to one indicates that the fraction w/y, which weights b_1' in (5), is nearly constant. Therefore b_1', will be unbiased as w varies.

On the other hand, the regression coefficient of log w on log y_n is only 0.11.[4] For when the wife's earnings increase in percentage terms, the income from non-labor sources is increasing by a good deal more in percentage terms. Thus, the fraction w/y_n (or $W\hat{M}/Y_n$) is decreasing, deflating the "true" income elasticity or, in other words, biasing the income elasticity toward zero. To compensate for this bias, we can multiply the income elasticity term, a_1', by the reciprocal of the estimate of $d \log w / d \log y_n$ (=0.11). The reciprocal is 9, and this blows up the estimate of the substitution elasticity in equation (4) to 3.52, which jumps out of the range of our other estimates.[5]

It has been noted, for example, that the elasticity coefficient of the wife's earnings, $b_2' = 1.01$, is a lower bound. And we expect equation (5), in which $a_3' = 1.37$ (or 1.35 if w/y is allowed to vary according to the estimating equation of w on y), to give us an upper bound, since the cross-elasticity of the husband's wage, a_2', is assumed to be less than or equal to zero. Any negative value of a_2' would decrease the absolute value of the income elasticity term that is added to the coefficient (b_2') of the wife's wage variable to get the substitution effect (a_3').

[3] I am indebted to Marvin Kosters for this point.

[4] The arithmetic regression coefficients of w on y is 0.69 and of w on y_n is 0.57. Thus each $100 increase in husband's income is associated with a $69 increase in the earnings of the wife, which just about keeps equal the ratio of w to y. The increase of $57 in w for each $100 increase in y_n, however, sharply decreases the ratio of w to y_n. There is a high correlation between w and y, .83 in both arithmetic and log forms. But the correlation between w and y_n is disturbingly low; .30 in arithmetic form and .24 in log form. This low degree of correlation will be referred to in the text.

[5] The solution of equation (4) is: $a_3' = 1.01 - (-.09)\ (3.1)\ (9) = 3.52$.

In this light, the estimate of a_3' from equation (4) that assumes that the ratio, w/y_n, is constant across SMA's is compatible with these lower and upper bounds. In addition to a general skepticism about the meaning of the variable y_n that has been expressed (see page 12), the particular difficulty with (4) when we attempt to estimate how w/y_n varies may lie in the poor fit (a correlation of only .2 to .3) between these two variables in the data.

Perhaps, then, we can consider the pure substitution elasticity to be around 1.25 with these data. Therefore, for each 1 per cent increase in wages, compensated by a 1 per cent decrease in family income, we could expect a 1.25 per cent increase in work rates by wives.

Let us turn to the remaining variables in the regressions in Table 11. A negative effect of the presence of children is expected, since this represents the demands for homework made upon the wife that, in turn, reflect the skills and tastes for homework as well as the unplanned births of children. A one per cent increase in c, the per cent of husband-wife families with 1 or more children under 18 years of age, is associated with a 1.2 per cent decrease in work rates of wives. The measure that gives the per cent of families with children under 6 years of age, c', is also significant and negative as shown in line 5. This measure appears, somewhat surprisingly, weaker than c, and when both measures were included in the same regression, only c held up in significance (regression not shown). I use the "stronger" variables in cases like this, where a choice appears arbitrary from the standpoint of my main interest in the economic aspects of the problem.

The variable for the male unemployment rate carries a significant, negative sign. One interpretation of this result is that the discouraging effect of depressed business conditions (which reduces the effective w) overpowers the stimulus to work caused by the sharp declines in family incomes in those households where male members (especially husbands) become unemployed. This issue, which involves the controversy over the "added" versus "discouraged" worker hypotheses, will be discussed in greater detail later in this chapter after the regression results for 1940 and 1960 have been presented. It is worth noting here, however, that the sign of u is, of course, a net effect over all families in the metropolitan area. The reduction in effective w affects nearly all wives who are in or potentially in the labor force, whereas the income-decline effect of u operates mainly on wives in families in which unemployment strikes.

The effect of education (e) is positive but not consistently significant. If, as I have suggested, education supplements the wage variable by serving as a proxy for non-pecuniary aspects, the effect is not consistently powerful with this body of data. Excluding e does raise the coefficient of w, and this suggests that both variables are playing similar roles in affecting wives' work rates.

Regressions on lines 3 and 4 show the results when the variables of lesser power, e and y_n, are dropped. The R^2 is nearly as large as it is when all the variables are included, and the coefficients of the remaining variables are only slightly altered.

Finally, regression 6 shows that the wage effect remains larger than the income effect when other variables are excluded, and this remains true when the regional variable is also dropped (regression not shown). The R^2 declined to 0.24 without r. The importance of the regional variable with these data is evident, but why it is important is not clear. This is one of several questions taken up in the next section.

Regression Results with Total Married Women with 1950 Census Data: Supplementary Results (Table 13)

Table 13 displays a mixed group of regressions that bring out some new points and shed light on the previous findings from different angles. In the first four lines of Table 13 the variable, w', measuring the median income earned for all females with income is included. This variable is useful as an aid in understanding the wage effect and also because it will facilitate comparisons of the 1950 results with the 1940 regressions for all wives and with the 1950 regressions covering data for nonwhite wives.

Line 1 shows that w' is much weaker as a determinant of m, the labor force participation of wives, than the full-time wage, w. The variable, w' is weaker despite a "mechanical" positive correlation between w' and m, derived from a positive relation between weeks worked by wives and w' and between weeks worked and m. The low effect of w' probably reflects its weakness as a proxy for the "true" wage. It is as if w' contains "errors" as a measure of the wage rate, and the error component biases the regression coefficient towards zero. Husband's income is positive (but statistically insignificant) in this regression, presumably because it is picking up the w effect in part.

Adding w' along with w and the complete set of variables of the model, as in lines 2 and 3, can indicate the effect of a wage proxy that applies to part-time female jobs—an important part of the employment opportunities for wives. About half of the females employed in 1949 worked less than 50–52 weeks.[6] Assume that the number of weeks or hours worked by the part-time workers among females does not vary much across areas.

[6] Bancroft reports that 55.8 per cent of employed females worked 12 months in 1949. Gertrude Bancroft, *The American Labor Force*, (New York: John Wiley, 1958), p. 101.

TABLE 13

REGRESSION RESULTS WITH TOTAL MARRIED WOMEN, 77 SMA'S IN 1950[a]

LINE	FORM[b]	R^2	Independent Variables										
			Constant	y	w	w'	y_n	r	c	u	e	n	ind
1...	A	.39	4.67	.31 (.18)	....	.60 (.20)	....	5.65 (.96)	....	....	....	....	....
2...	A	.68	32.48	−.56 (.21)	.72 (.26)	.59 (.19)	−.79 (.27)	3.76 (.86)	− .42 (.10)	−.26 (.19)	1.37 (.41)	....	....
3...	L	.67	3.40	−.71 (.30)	.75 (.24)	.29 (.12)	−.15 (.06)	.17 (.04)	−1.06 (.25)	−.08 (.05)	.54 (.21)	....	....
4...	A	.69	31.13	−.64 (.22)	.77 (.26)	.58 (.19)	−.69 (.28)	2.60 (1.25)	− .39 (.10)	−.30 (.20)	1.41 (.41)	.07 (.05)	....
5...	A	.62	38.02	−.31 (.21)	.98 (.23)	....	....	2.48 (.91)	− .35 (.09)	−.43 (.20)	....	....	−.13 (.03)
6...	L	.66	2.84	−.44 (.29)	.97 (.21)	....	....	.05 (.02)	− .96 (.23)	−.11 (.05)	....	....	−.24 (.08)
7...	L	.63	3.40	−.71 (.28)	1.00 (.22)	....	....	....	− .97 (.24)	−.15 (.04)	....	....	−.32 (.07)

[a] Dependent variable: labor force participation rate of married women, husband present.

[b] A = arithmetic; L = logarithmic.

Definitions of independent variables (see Appendix A for sources, means, and standard deviations)

- y median income for male family heads, spouse present, 1949 (hundreds of dollars)
- w median income of females who worked 50–52 weeks in 1949 (hundreds of dollars)
- w' median income of all females with income (hundreds of dollars)
- y_n referred to as non-labor income (hundreds of dollars). See Appendix A for full definition.
- r dummy variable for the region of the U.S.: "1" is a southern SMA; "0" otherwise
- e median years of schooling completed of females, 25 years and older
- u male unemployment rate (in per cent)
- c per cent of husband-wife families with one or more children under 18 years of age
- n the per cent nonwhite in the SMA
- ind the per cent of labor force in industries employing mostly male workers (see Appendix A for full definition)

Then the part-time earnings for each area may be considered a proxy for the wage rate, call it w_1, that part-time female workers earn. We can now give a rough interpretation of the total wage effects (for w and w' combined) in lines 2 to 4.

$$bw + cw' = bw + c(\tfrac{1}{2}w + \tfrac{1}{2}w_1) = (b + c/2)w + (c/2)w_1$$

Substituting the regression coefficients from line 2 of Table 13 for b and c, we have

$$1.015w + .295w_1$$

Note that in line 1 of Table 11, the regression corresponding to line 2 of Table 13, the coefficient of w is nearly identical to the value obtained as above from line 2. This interpretation of the coefficients of w and w_1 and the stronger education effect (again, compare lines 2–3 in Table 13 to lines 1–2 of Table 11) suggest that the use of w alone understates the wage or substitution effect. Note also that non-labor income has become statistically significant in the regressions with w and w'.

The regional variable, by itself, tells us little about the determinants of labor force participation. A first guess is that the positive sign of the dummy variable, r, where South = 1 and North = 0, reflects the higher participation rates of Negro wives, who are disproportionately southern residents. One test of this is given by including the variable, n, the per cent of the SMA population that is nonwhite, into the regression along with r. Regression 4 of Table 13 shows that r stays significant and positive, although reduced in size from 3.76 in line 2 to 2.60 in line 4, while n is insignificant. Without the regional variable (regressions not shown) n takes on its expected significant positive sign.

Another attempt to understand the causal factors implied by the regional variable involves the industrial structure of the two regions. It is common knowledge that the South is characterized by lighter industries that offer relatively more employment opportunities for women. The importance of the industrial structure of the area is borne out by an examination of residuals from the regressions. For the three census years for which regressions were run, metropolitan areas like Pittsburgh, Detroit, Gary, and Youngstown—all heavy industry areas—consistently had the largest negative residuals (that is, actual rate minus predicted rate), and light industry areas like Hartford, Reading, and Columbia, South Carolina had the extreme positive values.[7] The interpretation seems straightforward

[7] This point was made by Schoenberg and Douglas who noted that Fall River (a textile city) and Scranton (mining) had extreme high and low values, respectively, of labor force participation rates for females. Erika H. Schoenberg and Paul H. Douglas, "Studies in the Supply Curve of Labor," *The Journal of Political Economy*, XLV (1937),

when we recognize that, for example, the high female wage observed in Pittsburgh does not allow for the non-pecuniary disadvantages of the heavy work that is characteristic of the dominant steel industry in that city.

The analysis of residuals led to another interesting and somewhat contrasting conclusion. For matched cities and SMA's from census to census, the residuals from the fitted regressions were very weakly correlated. Thus, despite the consistency of the largest residuals, plus or minus, for the few SMA's like Hartford and Pittsburgh, across *all* the SMA's the pattern of residuals showed an unsystematic scatter. This would indicate that either the industrial structure does not vary much across most of the SMA's or that it changed from decade to decade. Also implied is that the "left-out" variables that are systematically related to the SMA's do not appear to be correlated with labor force participation rates of wives, given the presence in the model of the variables I have used.

To get a measure of this factor a variable, *ind*, was defined as the per cent of the civilian labor force in an area which is employed in industries that are "heavy demanders of male labor." (See Appendix B, Table 42 for the source and derivation of *ind*.) The six industries so characterized had female employment percentages that ranged from a low of 2.4 per cent in mining to a high of 15.9 per cent in durable manufacturing. The variable, *ind*, has, of course, a strong negative relation to the labor force participation rate of married women. The simple correlation between *m* and *ind* was −.58. Also important in this context is its negative relation to the regional variable. The simple correlation between *r* and *ind* was −.44.

The result of adding *ind* is shown by regressions 5–7. In comparing lines 5 and 6 here to lines 3 and 4 of Table 11, we see that the addition of *ind* reduces *r* from 3.55 to 2.48 (or .07 to .05 in logs). When *r* is left out, as in 7, *ind* is one of several variables to improve in explanatory power, and the R^2 in 7 is only slightly reduced from that in 6. It is noteworthy that all the other variables in the regressions from Table 11 retain their general magnitudes and relationships after *ind* is added, except for *w*, where the reduction is expected since *ind* also represents a demand factor.

Regression Results with Total Married Women with 1940 Census Data: Main Results (Table 14)

For 1940 the most complete data are available for cities rather than metropolitan areas. These should be comparable to the 1950 and 1960

p. 65. See also Nedra B. Belloc, "Labor Force Participation and Employment Opportunities of Women," *Journal of the American Statistical Association*, XLV (September, 1950) for similar findings.

SMA data, however. Although by 1950 the suburban growth around cities, the location of plants in suburbs, and the widespread ownership of the automobile made the SMA the appropriate designation of a "labor market," in 1940 the city should adequately represent this economic entity.[8]

The income and earnings variables available for 1940 are considerably different and less satisfactory compared to 1950 or 1960. The amount of income from non-labor sources was not collected in the 1940 census, so this variable is not used.[9] The income variable, y', applies to all males with income in 1939 rather than to husbands. The earnings for females, w', is not for full-time workers but for all females with income in 1939.

Despite these differences the results shown in Table 14 generally support the 1950 results. The wage effect is positive and the income effect negative. The variables for children and unemployment again are significant and negative. Education becomes significant and positive and the wage effect larger when the unemployment rate is dropped (line 4); and when e, u, and c'' are all excluded, the wage rate coefficient increases to a point where its elasticity measure exceeds the income elasticity in absolute value (lines 6–8). Both income and wage coefficients are insignificant when the regional variable is not present, and the R^2 declines to .13 (regression not shown).

The important difference between the regressions for 1940 and those for 1950 lies in the variable representing the wage rate.[10] We have seen in Table 13 that the "all earnings" wage variable, w', is decidedly inferior to the full-time earnings variable, w. The simple correlation between the two, incidentally, was only .6 in 1950 for all 77 SMA's and .4 for the 57 non-southern SMA's. These considerations suggest that if a measure of full-time female earnings were available, the wage effect would be increased relative to the income effect for the 1940 data.

Regression Results with Total Married Women with 1960 Data: Main Results (Table 15)

The 1960 census offers the largest number of observations for the regression analysis. There are 100 standard statistical metropolitan areas

[8] The changing character of cities and metropolitan areas during the ten-year period from 1940 to 1950 is discussed in Amos H. Hawley, *The Changing Shapes of Metropolitan America* (Glencoe: The Free Press, 1956).

[9] William G. Bowen and T. Aldrich Finegan have made use of a variable measuring the per cent of families in the city who reported receiving some non-labor income during 1939. Their results with this variable suggest that it does serve as a proxy for the amount of non-labor income. See Bowen and Finegan, "Labor Force Participation and Unemployment," in *Employment Policy and the Labor Market*, ed. A. M. Ross (Berkeley and Los Angeles: University of California Press, 1965).

[10] Median earnings for all males (y') is, statistically, a close substitute for husbands' earnings (y). The simple correlation between the two is .9 for 1950, and trials with both indicate little difference in their effects in the multiple regressions for 1950.

in the continental United States with 250,000 population or more. (Honolulu was excluded because the nonwhite population there is large and almost entirely Oriental rather than Negro.)

The variables available from this census are about the same as for the 1950 census. An important exception is the measure of income from non-labor sources. For 1950 the variable was published as the median amount of non-labor income per adult recipient of this type of income. The average over all SMA's was about $650. In 1960, however, the per capita amount of non-labor income was obtained on the basis of the aggregate

TABLE 14

REGRESSION RESULTS WITH TOTAL MARRIED WOMEN, 41 CITIES IN 1940[a]

LINE	FORM[b]	R^2	INDEPENDENT VARIABLES						
			Constant	y'	w'	r	c''	u	e
1	A	.81	42.86	−1.02 (.38)	1.32 (.45)	4.55 (1.11)	−.94 (.16)	−.43 (.15)	.11 (.40)
2	.....	.....	.....	−.73[c]	.54[c]	.....	.....	.....	.....
3	L	.76	3.63	−.53 (.25)	.31 (.20)	.08 (.03)	−1.27 (.22)	−.38 (.12)	.04 (.24)
4	L	.69	2.62	−.59 (.28)	.39 (.22)	.13 (.03)	−1.16 (.25)	.....	.43 (.22)
5	L	.66	3.02	−.49 (.29)	.42 (.23)	.13 (.03)	−1.25 (.25)	.....	.....
6	A	.52	8.29	−.59 (.55)	1.96 (.67)	7.99 (1.45)	.....	.....	.....
7	.....	.....	.....	−.40[c]	.80[c]	.....	.....	.....	.....
8	L	.42	.92	−.23 (.37)	.58 (.30)	.19 (.04)	.....	.....	.....

[a] Dependent variable: labor force participation rate of married women, husband present.
[b] A = arithmetic; L = logarithmic.
[c] Elasticities at the mean.
Definitions of independent variables (see Appendix A for sources, means, and standard deviations)
y' median income of all males with income, 1939 (hundreds of dollars)
w' median income of all females with income, 1939 (hundreds of dollars)
r dummy variable for the region of the U.S.: "1" is a southern city; "0" otherwise
c'' number of children under 5 years of age per 100 women ever married
u male unemployment rate (in per cent)
e median years of schooling completed of females, 25 years and older

amount of this type of income divided by all persons in the area who received any kind of income in 1959.[11] The average of this measure over all 100 metropolitan areas was $423. It is less in 1960 than in 1950 because, roughly speaking, the 1960 non-labor income was spread over the whole population, whereas in 1950 it was measured as the average amount just among recipients. The latter measure, for 1950, is the preferred one.[12]

Another change in variables from 1950 to 1960 concerns the measure for the presence of children. In 1960 c''' measures the number of children

[11] I am indebted to Bowen and Finegan for their discovery of this measure among the 1960 census materials and for sending the figures to me. See their use of this measure in Bowen and Finegan, *op. cit.*

[12] Just as we want the wage rate variable for the model to measure the earnings of females who worked, so we would like the measure of non-labor income to be based on those who receive this type of income. The "second best" nature of the 1960 measure was expressed to me by T. Aldrich Finegan in correspondence.

TABLE 15

REGRESSION RESULTS WITH TOTAL MARRIED WOMEN, SMA'S IN 1960[a]

	LINE	FORM[b]	R^2	Con-stant	y	w	y_n	r	c'''	u	e
				INDEPENDENT VARIABLES							
Total United States, 100 SMA's	1	L	.53	2.74	−.68 (.17)	.42 (.15)	−.27 (.06)	.01 (.03)	−.77 (.16)	−.07 (.03)	.53 (.15)
	2	L	.47	2.81	−.55 (.17)	.52 (.16)	−.20 (.06)	.04 (.03)	−.66 (.16)	−.08 (.03)	....
	3	A	.37	33.67	−.29 (.11)	.34 (.17)	....	1.47 (.95)	−.61 (.20)	−.13 (.08)	1.32 (.54)
	4	L	.43	2.56	−.52 (.18)	.38 (.17)	....	.02 (.01)	−.42 (.15)	−.12 (.03)	.30 (.15)
	5	A	.18	23.44	−.24 (.13)	.62 (.17)	....	3.27 (.97)	....	....	....
	6	L	.19	1.14	−.39 (.21)	.67 (.18)	....	.05 (.01)	....	....	....
North only, 71 SMA's	7	A	.42	58.74	−.45 (.13)	.34 (.18)	....	....	−.11 (.02)	−.04 (.07)	1.04 (.48)
Less than 10 per cent nonwhite population: 60 SMA's	8	L	.49	3.70	−.74 (.24)	.47 (.21)	....	....	−.82 (.21)	−.07 (.03)	.32 (.20)
	9	L	.46	3.60	−.61 (.23)	.54 (.21)	....	....	−.77 (.21)	−.08 (.03)	....
	10	L	.19	1.03	−.40 (.27)	.75 (.25)	....	....	....	....	....

[a] Dependent variable: labor force participation rate of married women, husband present.

[b] A = arithmetic; L = logarithmic.

Definitions of independent variables (see Appendix A for sources, means, and standard deviations)

- y median income for male family heads, spouse present, 1959 (hundreds of dollars)
- w median income of females who worked 50–52 weeks in 1959 (hundreds of dollars)
- y_n referred to as non-labor income (hundreds of dollars). See Appendix A for full definition.
- r dummy variable for the region of the U.S.: "1" is a southern SMA; "0" otherwise
- c''' number of children ever born per 1,000 women ever married
- u male unemployment rate (in per cent)
- e median years of schooling completed of females, 25 years and older

under 18 years of age per woman ever married. In 1950 c was the per cent of females with children under 18 years of age. In 1960, as in 1950, the variable c', the percent of families with children under 6 years of age, was used and found to be weaker than the alternative measure.

Results from the basic regression model with the 1960 data generally agree with the results of the 1950 and 1940 censuses, but there are some notable differences. As with 1950, the log form of the regressions gives the best over-all fit (see Table 15).

The relative sizes of the wage and income variables in 1960 behave in a manner similar to those in 1940. Unlike the results for 1950 the income elasticity is larger in absolute value than the wage elasticity (except in lines 5 and 6 when the supplementary variables are excluded). Since the same proxies for the husband's income and wife's wage are used in 1960 as in 1950 the absolute decline in w (from over 1 to around $\frac{1}{2}$) and the decline in w relative to y cannot be attributed to the use of different empirical constructs as they could in 1940.

The variable for the education of the wife is more significant in 1960 than in 1950 or 1940. I would speculate that this may be part of the reason for the decline in the coefficient of w in 1960—that e is playing a more important role as a wage-effect proxy than it did previously. This could be explained by the growing importance in the female labor force of white collar occupations, where formal educational attainment represents the skills demanded and stands as a proxy for pleasant working conditions and appealing work.

Non-labor income appears highly significant and has its expected negative sign. The children and unemployment variables again have significant, negative coefficients. (Unemployment is significant only when the log form of the regression is used.)[13] The regional variable appears much less important for 1960, but this might be expected since the North and South have grown more similar with respect to race and nativity composition and industrial structure in the past 20 years.

Two additional sets of regressions are included in Table 15: one for the 71 northern SMA's and the other for 60 SMA's in which nonwhites comprised less than 10 per cent of the population in 1960. Both sets should

[13] The arithmetic value of the male unemployment rate in the 1960 regression performed weakly as a consequence of several large rates of over 10 per cent (in the Johnstown and Wilkes-Barre areas of Pennsylvania and Duluth, Minnesota). These points were "off" the regression plane. The logarithmic form, of course, reduces the "importance" of the very large values in determining a linear fit. The simple correlation between the arithmetic values of the male unemployment rate and the female unemployment rate was only .16, and the correlation between the male unemployment rate and the per cent of males who worked less than 50–52 weeks in 1959 was .17. The correlations between these variables in logarithmic form are .50 and .38, respectively.

reveal the sort of results that would apply to samples restricted to white married women. Generally, the results are similar to those for the United States as a whole. Compare, for example, lines 3 and 7, lines 4 and 8, and lines 6 and 10. (The regional variable is properly missing from lines 8, 9, and 10 since either none or only a few of the southern SMA's are involved.)

Before leaving this group of regressions, it is instructive to compute income and substitution elasticities and compare them with those from the 1950 data. The two equations for this purpose are:

$$a_3' = b_2' - a_1' \left(\frac{W\hat{M}}{Y_n}\right) \quad (4)$$

$$a_3' = b_2' - b_1' \left(\frac{W\hat{M}}{Y\hat{Q}}\right) \quad (5)$$

Using the appropriate log coefficients from line 1 of Table 15 and ratios of mean values for earnings and income figures, we have:

$$a_3' = .42 - (-.27)(7.6) = 2.47 \quad (4)$$

$$a_3' = .42 - (-.68)(.61) = .83 \quad (5)$$

The regression on line 2 drops e and permits the wage variable to pick up the effects of the education variable; this yields values for a_3' of 2.04 and .87 for (4) and (5), respectively.

These computations lead to a more serious inconsistency than was the case with the 1950 results. Here the upper boundary for an estimate of the substitution elasticity that is given by (5) is substantially less than the estimate from equation (4). In 1950 (4) was larger than (5) only after the two estimates were weighted by reciprocals of the coefficients expressing the relative change in wife's earnings with respect to the relative change in the appropriate income variable. And this inconsistency was perhaps explained by the lack of any strong relationship between w and y_n, which made suspect weighting by the reciprocal of $(d \log w)/(d \log y_n)$ that gave rise to the problem.

Using weights to compensate for changes in the ratios of w to y and y_n (as w changes) with the equations above exacerbates the problem. The ratio of w to y is again fairly constant across SMA's, so the weighted ratio does not much change a_3' in (5).[14] However, the weight for the ratio of w to y_n is 5, and this enlarges the estimate from equation (4) to 11.67.[15]

[14] The coefficient of log w regressed on log y is 0.95, making the weight 1.05, so the new estimate of a_3' from (5) is .85. The simple correlation between w and y for the 1960 data is .85 and the arithmetic regression coefficient is 0.58. All these values are similar to those of 1950.

[15] The coefficient of log w on log y_n is 0.20. The simple correlation between w and y_n is only .22.

Two disturbing elements with the weighted computation here are that: first, y_n again is weakly correlated with w; secondly, the ratio w/y_n may be excessively large because the procedure for obtaining y_n gave relatively small values for this variable.

Equation (5) gives us a more conservative and, I believe, a more accurate estimate of the substitution elasticity. With the 1950 data a_3' was around 1.25, and it is lower, around 0.80, in 1960.

Tests of the Added Worker Hypothesis and Supplementary Tests with Census Data

The sets of regressions for each of the census years, 1940, 1950, and 1960, have consistently shown the effect of the male unemployment rate in the city or metropolitan area to be significantly negative on the labor force participation rate of wives. The issues raised by this finding are related in an important way to labor force behavior during the business cycle. Wives are the largest group among the "secondary workers"[16] in the American economy, and the labor force participation, or lack of it, of secondary workers with respect to swings in the business cycle will largely determine the size of the labor force in the short run. Primary workers, like the heads of families or single men aged 20 to 60, are firmly attached to the labor force over the short run, although they, of course, may move in and out of the status of employed or unemployed.

In this section a closer scrutiny will be made of the question of whether the net effect of unemployment serves to expand or contract the labor force. The theoretical underpinnings of the question have already been outlined. A high unemployment rate indicates that large numbers of the principal breadwinners are out of work or are working "short hours," that the incomes of their families are undergoing transitory declines, and that to make up this income loss other adults in the family enter the labor

[16] Secondary workers commonly refer to workers in a family unit who are not the main earner and/or to workers who, regardless of family status, have a casual or part-time commitment to the labor force. The following categories more or less cover the secondary-worker group, and the numbers (in millions) in parentheses tell how many were in the labor force during March, 1964 (source: U.S. Department of Labor, Bureau of Labor Statistics, Special Labor Force Report, No. 50, p. A-8):

Married women, husband present (14.5)
Single women, aged 14–19 (2.3)
Single women, aged 55 and over (0.6)
Females of other marital status, aged 55 and over (1.9)
Males, aged 65 and over (2.1)
Single men, aged 14–19 (3.0)

Two points of interest about these numbers are that: (1) together these six categories comprise almost 33 per cent of the total labor force; and (2) wives make up about 60 per cent of the total number of secondary workers by this definition.

force. At the same time a high unemployment rate indicates an unfavorable market for the sellers of labor. A person entering the labor force is likely to experience a longer period of waiting and search for a job, or accept a less attractive job, or both. There are, then, plus and minus factors involved and the net effect of unemployment is not clear a priori.

A more formal statement of the theory may be made within the framework of Model I that handles the cross-section aggregative data for SMA's and cities. Restricting the model to the income and earnings variables—y, husband's income, representing a normal or permanent concept of income, and w, the wife's full-time wage—we have:

$$m = b_1 y + b_2 w \tag{1}$$

Let the transitory or cyclical changes in the earnings figures be y_t and w_t, which will reflect the current state of the market. Then:

$$m = b_1 y + b_2 w + a_1 y_t + a_2 w_t \tag{2}$$

where we expect $a_1 < 0$ and $a_2 > 0$.

It is reasonable to suppose that the unemployment rate, u, will represent large portions of the transitory changes in income and, in addition, will capture some of the non-wage adjustments to changes in employment conditions—tightening or relaxing hiring standards, work assignments, and the like.[17] As an approximation:

$$y_t = \alpha u \tag{3}$$

$$w_t = \beta u \tag{4}$$

where α and β are unemployment-adjustment coefficients that are both expected to be negative. Substituting (3) and (4) in (2):

$$m = b_1 y + b_2 w + b_3 u \qquad \text{where} \qquad b_3 = (\alpha a_1 + \beta a_2) \tag{5}$$

and b_3 will be positive or negative as αa_1 is greater or less than $/\beta a_2/$.[18]

[17] See Melvin W. Reder, "A Theory of Occupational Wage Differentials," *American Economic Review*, XLV (December, 1955) for a discussion of this point.

[18] One might question whether y faithfully represents a "permanent" or "normal" concept of income. The variation in u across areas may suggest that a transitory component is included in y. In this case $y = y_c = y_p + y_t$ where y_c is current, reported income and y_p is, of course, the permanent component. Instead of $y_p = y$ we have $y_p = y - y_t$ and this enters equation (2) as follows:

$$m = b_1(y - y_t) + b_2 w + a_1 y_t + a_2 w_t \tag{2'}$$

so that equation (5) becomes:

$$m = b_1 y + b_2 w + b_3 u \qquad \text{where} \qquad b_3 = (\alpha a_1 + \beta a_2 - \alpha b_1) \tag{5'}$$

What (5′) says about the coefficient, b_3, is that unemployment represents more than

This interpretation of b_3 shows that the sign and size of the effect of u will depend on the relative magnitude of the adjustment factors, α and β, relating y_t and w_t to u, as well as on the effects, a_1 and a_2, of the transitory components. The discussion that follows about the effects of u in terms of transitory income and wage effects implicitly assumes near equality in the magnitude of α and β. This assumption is not necessary, but is made for the convenience of discussion.

The effects of y, w, and u on m have been incorporated in a model with other variables, as we have seen. Table 16 brings together some of the regression results from the previous tables,[19] and adds two regressions (lines 4 and 7) that substitute a variable, y_{52}, median income of males who worked 50 to 52 weeks in the year preceding, as an income proxy relatively free of transitory components occasioned by unemployment (see footnote 18, page 63).

The main point of Table 16 from the standpoint of this section is that the net effect of unemployment on the labor force participation of wives is significantly negative for all three census years. For 1940 and 1950 the arithmetic coefficient of u is approximately -0.50. Thus, a rise in unemployment rates of 2 percentage points, say from 4 per cent to 6 per cent, would be associated with a decrease of 1 percentage point in labor force participation rates, say from 30 per cent to 29 per cent. On a base of about 40 million wives in 1960, the number in the labor force would decline from 12 million to 11.6 million. The logarithmic coefficient (-0.12) in the largest regression for 1960 has a similar effect. A 50 per cent increase in unemployment, again from 4 per cent to 6 per cent, would decrease labor force participation rates by 6 per cent. And a decline of this magnitude, say from a participation rate of 30 per cent to 28.2 per cent, would decrease

---

just the effects of transitory changes in y and w; that high unemployment (for given, reported y) represents normally higher y_p, and it is this fact that contributes to a low (or negative) effect of u; that low unemployment represents normally lower y_p, and this fact contributes to the high (or positive) effect of u.

The empirical question is whether y is a good proxy for y_p. As a test of this specification problem, I will use in several regressions, y_{52}, the median earnings of males who worked 50 to 52 weeks a year. This corresponds to w. Both y_{52} and w should be relatively insensitive to u—or each sensitive in somewhat offsetting ways—with respect to the labor force participation of wives. It turns out that very similar results are obtained with y_{52} as with y.

[19] There are two differences between Table 16 and Tables 11–15. First, the constant term is not reproduced in Table 16 as it adds nothing to the discussion in this context. Second, the variable for non-labor income, y_n, is not included. It was not available in 1940 and not consistently significant in 1950. When y_n was included in the regressions with 1950 and 1960 data, however, the effect of unemployment was still negative, as can be seen in Tables 11 and 15.

TABLE 16

REGRESSION RESULTS WITH TOTAL MARRIED WOMEN, 1940, 1950, AND 1960[a]

YEAR	LINE	FORM[b]	R^2	INDEPENDENT VARIABLES						
				y	y_{52}	w	c	r	e	u
1940 (41 cities)	1	A	.81	−1.02 (.38)	....	1.32 (.45)	−.94 (.16)	4.55 (1.11)	.11 (.40)	−.43 (.15)
	2	L	.76	−.53 (.25)	....	.31 (.20)	−1.27 (.22)	.08 (.03)	.04 (.24)	−.38 (.12)
1950 (77 SMA's)	3	A	.55	−.53 (.24)	....	1.21 (.27)	−.31 (.12)	3.57 (.99)	.56 (.40)	−.55 (.22)
1950 (77 SMA's)	4	A	.60	....	−.34 (.17)	1.06 (.19)	−.42 (.09)	3.40 (.94)	....	−.44 (.22)
1950 Non-southern (57 SMA's)	5	A	.56	−.84 (.31)	....	1.48 (.35)	−.53 (.16)	....	.95 (.45)	−.56 (.26)
1960 (100 SMA's)	6	L	.43	−.52 (.18)	....	.38 (.17)	−.42 (.15)	.02 (.01)	.30 (.15)	−.12 (.03)
1960 (100 SMA's)	7	L	.42	....	−.39 (.15)	.25 (.15)	−.38 (.15)	.05 (.03)	.30 (.15)	−.11 (.03)
1960 (60 SMA's with nonwhite <10%)	8	L	.49	−.74 (.24)	....	.47 (.21)	−.82 (.21)	....	.32 (.20)	−.07 (.03)

[a] Dependent variables: labor force participation rate of married women, husband present.

[b] A = arithmetic; L = logarithmic.

Definitions of independent variables (see Appendix A for sources, means, and standard deviations)

y median income for male family heads, spouse present, for the year preceding that of the census (hundreds of dollars)

y_{52} median income of males who worked 50–52 weeks in the year preceding the census (hundreds of dollars)

w median income of females who worked 50–52 weeks in the year preceding the census (hundreds of dollars)

c (The variable for the presence of children has slightly different definitions for the three census years: c'' for 1940, c for 1950, and c''' for 1960. See Tables 11 to 15)

r dummy variable for the region of the U.S.: "1" is a southern SMA or city; "0" otherwise

e median years of schooling completed of females, 25 years and older

u male unemployment rate (in per cent)

the number of wives in the labor force from 12 million to about 11.3 million. We do not know, however, what length of time is required for these responses in labor force participation. The effects are based on cross-sectional and therefore static models, so we could not state with confidence that a decline in unemployment would, say, after six months, produce the rise in labor force participation predicted by the regressions reported here. Before assessing the validity of these findings, I should like to subject the model to some additional tests.

Tests with the 1950 Data

Table 17 examines the 1950 data with several additional variables that serve to check on the unemployment effect. In line 1 of Table 17 the per cent of males employed less than 27 weeks in 1949 (u') is substituted for the unemployment rate in the census week of 1950 (u). If, as seems plausible, the response of wives to unemployment of their husbands is delayed for several weeks or several months, then this measure should permit a positive effect to show up. Instead we see that the coefficient of u' is negative and even larger and more significant than that of u (see line 2, Table 11). The reason for this is not clear. Perhaps u' is a better measure of depressed business conditions. We should remember, however, that u' is not a "pure" unemployment measure. It includes among those who worked less than 27 weeks, new entrants to the labor force and part-time workers as well as those unemployed this length of time. Perhaps larger numbers of part-year workers, who may well be good substitutes for wives in the labor market, cause lower participation rates among wives. For the 1960 tests a variable is used for the unemployment experience in 1959 that largely avoids this problem.

Another check on the interpretation of the effect of unemployment is provided by the regression on line 2. The variable, *ind*, that measures the industrial structure of the metropolitan area is added to test whether the negative signs of u and u' simply reflect the concentration of the cyclically sensitive, heavy industries that have a low demand for female labor. The claim might be made that unemployment tended to be high in the very cities where heavy industries are preponderant and that, for this reason, would tend to have low participation rates among wives. We see, however, that the coefficient of u' is only slightly diminished. The negative effect persists, and the same result was true with respect to u when *ind* was an added variable in Table 13.

As a final check on the unemployment effect the female unemployment rate, u_f, was included in the regression. Because the dependent variable is defined as the employment rate of wives *plus their unemployment rate*, there is a "mechanical" relation between m and u_f correlating the two positively.[20] It appears that the "economic" relation actually dominates so that (in line 3) the coefficient of u_f is negative. When both male and female unemployment rates are included, as in line 4, the collinearity between them reduces both coefficients to smaller sizes than their standard errors.

TABLE 17

REGRESSION RESULTS WITH TOTAL MARRIED WOMEN, 77 SMA'S IN 1950[a]

LINE	FORM[b]	R^2	INDEPENDENT VARIABLES									
			y	w	y_n	r	c	u	u'	u_f	e	*ind*
1....	L	.71	—1.29	1.29	—.09	.13	—1.01	......	—.46	......	.27	......
			(.33)	(.22)	(.05)	(.04)	(.23)	......	(.10)	......	(.17)	......
2....	L	.73	— .95	1.11)	—.13	.11	—1.00	......	—.39	......	.18	—.19
			(.35)	(.22)	(.06)	(.04)	(.23)	......	(.10)	......	(.17)	(.08)
3....	L	.61	— .52	1.21	......	.08	—1.09	......	......	—.091	......	......
			(.29)	(.23)	......	(.02)	(.24)	......	......	(.046)	......	......
4....	L	.62	— .59	1.20	......	.08	—1.09	—.065	......	—.047	......	......
			(.30)	(.23)	......	(.02)	(.29)	(.072)	......	(.067)	......	......

[a] Dependent variable: labor force participation rate of married women, husband present.
[b] A = arithmetic; L = logarithmic.

Definitions of independent variables (see Appendix A for sources, means, and standard deviations)

- y median income for male family heads, spouse present, 1949 (hundreds of dollars)
- w median income of females who worked 50–52 weeks in 1949 (hundreds of dollars)
- y_n referred to as non-labor income (hundreds of dollars). See Appendix A for full definition.
- r dummy variable for the region of the U.S.: "1" is a southern SMA; "0" otherwise
- c per cent of husband-wife families with one or more children under 18 years of age
- u male unemployment rate (in per cent)
- u' per cent of the male labor force who worked less than 27 weeks in 1949
- u_f female unemployment rate (in per cent)
- e median years of schooling completed by females 25 years and older.
- *ind* the per cent of the civilian labor force engaged in mining, construction, agriculture and related industries, business and repair services, transportation, communication, and durable manufacturing industries

Tests with the 1960 Data

The census data from 1960 are used for the regressions in Table 18. The first three lines cover cases that are similar to those tested with the 1950 data. Lines 1 and 2 in Table 18 show the significantly negative effect of unemployment when measured by the female unemployment rate, u_f. The male unemployment rate is not significant in arithmetic value (see

[20] There is likely to be an offset in the other direction, however. Mincer has called attention to a potential source of a spurious negative correlation between the labor force participation rate of a group of workers and their unemployment rate. The number in the labor force of the group is in the numerator of the dependent variable, and the same number is in the denominator of the unemployment rate for that group. To the degree that errors of measurement affect the labor force, a spurious negative correlation results. See Mincer, "Labor Force Participation and Unemployment: A Review of Recent Evidence." Mincer suggested that the negative spuriousness could be avoided by deflating both the labor force and the number of unemployed by the total population eligible to be in the labor force. When I performed this test with 1960 data, the negative effect of unemployment remained significant and as large as before. See lines 4 and 5 of Table 18.

TABLE 18

REGRESSION RESULTS WITH TOTAL MARRIED WOMEN, SMA'S IN 1960[a]

LINE	FORM[b]	R^2	INDEPENDENT VARIABLES													
			y	w	y_n	r	c'''	e	u	u_f	u''	u_t	ΔL	Δp	a_{65}	mg
1[c]....	A	.54	−.50	.48	−1.83	....	−.10	1.46	....	−.56	....	....	....	....	....	....
			(.09)	(.14)	(.36)	....	(.02)	(.40)	....	(.22)						
2[c]....	L	.53	−.74	.47	−.29	....	−.80	.50	....	−.10	....	....	....	....	....	....
			(.16)	(.15)	(.06)	....	(.14)	(.15)	....	(.04)						
3[c]....	A	.60	−.46	.39	−1.61	.34	−.09	1.20	....	....	−.19	....	....	....	....	....
			(.09)	(.13)	(.35)	(.77)	(.02)	(.39)	....		(.04)					
4[c]....	A	.59	−.50	.46	−1.52	....	−.07	1.29	....	....	....	−1.11	....	....	....	....
			(.09)	(.13)	(.35)	....	(.02)	(.38)	....			(.20)				
5[c]....	L	.58	−.71	.44	−.23	....	−.61	.44	....	....	....	−.16	....	....	....	....
			(.15)	(.14)	(.06)	....	(.15)	(.14)	....			(.04)				
6[c]....	L	.48	−.40	.34	....	.05	−.39	.30	−.15	....	....	....	....	−.06	....	.07
			(.18)	(.16)	....	(.03)	(.15)	(.19)	(.03)					(.02)		(.03)
7[c]....	L	.53	−.66	.43	−.27	.02	−.72	.53	−.07	....	....	....	....	....	.02	....
			(.18)	(.16)	(.07)	(.04)	(.19)	(.15)	(.03)						(.07)	
8[d]....	L	.49	−.64	.35	−.26	.05	−.64	.47	−.08	....	....	....	.00	....	....	....
			(.18)	(.17)	(.07)	(.03)	(.16)	(.15)	(.03)				(.29)			
9[d]....	A	.46	−.44	.34	−2.29	.04	−.11	1.48	−.06	....	....	....	.03	....	....	....
			(.11)	(.16)	(.46)	(.10)	(.02)	(.43)	(.07)				(.09)			

[a] Dependent variable: labor force participation rate of married women, husband present.

[b] A = arithmetic; L = logarithmic.

[c] 100 SMA's.

[d] 90 SMA's for which data were available on total non-agricultural employment for both 1959 and 1960.

Definitions of independent variables (see Appendix A for sources, means, and standard deviations)

- y median income for male family heads, spouse present, 1959 (hundreds of dollars)
- w median income of females who worked 50–52 weeks in 1959 (hundreds of dollars)
- y_n referred to as non-labor income (hundreds of dollars). See Appendix A for full definition.
- r dummy variable for the region of the U.S.: "1" is a southern SMA; "0" otherwise
- c''' number of children born per 1,000 women ever married.
- e median years of schooling completed of females, 25 years and older
- u male unemployment rate (in per cent)
- u_f female unemployment rate in 1960 (in per cent)
- u'' per cent of males, aged 35 to 44, who worked less than 50 weeks in 1959
- u_t ratio of the number of unemployed males to the total number of males eligible to be in the labor force
- ΔL percentage change in total non-agricultural employment in the SMA from 1959 to 1960
- Δp percentage change in population of the SMA from 1950 to 1960
- a_{65} per cent of the population in the SMA 65 years of age or older
- mg the per cent of the population who are in-migrants (i.e., lived in a different county five years ago)

footnote 13, p. 60), but it is in logarithmic values. When both male and female unemployment rates are entered in log form, collinearity between them again reduces the coefficients to insignificance (regression not shown).

On line 3, the tightness or looseness of the labor market is measured by u'', the per cent of prime-age males, 35–44, who worked less than 50 weeks in 1959. Like the variable u' used with the 1950 data, the effect is negative and larger in absolute value than the coefficient of the unemployment rate. Moreover, the weeks-worked experience of this age group of males will primarily reflect unemployment experience. With the 1950 data the variable used for all male workers, u', included the effects of entries and departures of other secondary workers, like teen-age males or elderly males.

The regressions in lines 4–5 use an unemployment rate defined as the number of unemployed males divided by the total number of males eligible to be in the labor force of the SMA. This definition avoids any negative spurious relation between a labor force participation rate that has the labor force in the numerator and an unemployment rate that has the labor force in the denominator (see footnote 20, p. 67). The newly defined unemployment rate also carries a significantly negative coefficient, and the coefficient of the variable, log u_t, permits a comparison with the conventional rate, u, that is independent of the units of measure. Comparing lines 5 and 6, no essential difference is indicated. When an unemployment rate for the civilian labor force was defined with the total eligible population in the denominator, the effect was also negative (regression not shown).

The last four lines of Table 18 (regressions 6–9) may be discussed as a group. These give special attention to the dynamic forces that affect the labor market and that may have been entering the model by way of the wage and unemployment variables, in particular.

Consider the case of a metropolitan area that experiences economic growth sustained over a period of months. It is likely that the tighter labor markets that ensue will be accompanied by the following events: (1) a reduction in the rate of unemployment and a rise in wages that entices wives and other secondary workers to enter the labor market; (2) a lowering of hiring standards that facilitates the recruitment of secondary workers;[21] (3) in-migration of persons eager to obtain jobs and who are attracted from other areas by events (1) and (2) above.[22]

[21] See Reder, *op. cit.*

[22] This is another point that Mincer made in his article, "Labor Force Participation and Unemployment: A Review of Recent Evidence."

Now, the correlation between the labor force participation rate and low unemployment and/or high wages may be reflecting the short-run dynamic events described by events (2) and (3). A long-run rise in wages offered to wives, for example, over the economy as a whole might well be less strongly related to increases in labor force participation than the wage increase that reflects labor conditions in one particular market, to which "eager workers" can migrate. It may also be true that unemployment associated with the normal ups and downs in the business activity of a stationary economy may have a weaker effect than unemployment that represents a high growth (or, conversely, a declining) market.

Although I cannot hope to explore adequately in this study the short-run dynamics of the labor market, it is possible to introduce a few variables to the model that offer some preliminary tests. The variables selected for the tests with 1960 data are: the percentage change in population of the SMA from 1950 to 1960, Δp; the per cent of the population over 5 years of age in 1960 who moved into the SMA during the last 5 years, mg; the per cent of the population 65 years of age and older, a_{65} (as a proxy for an aged population); the percentage change in total non-agricultural employment in the SMA from 1959 to 1960, ΔL.[23]

As shown in Table 18 this group of variables serving as proxies for growth and employment change do not have a pronounced effect on the basic wage, income, and unemployment variables. The log coefficient of w moves around 0.35 as it did in Table 15 when a large number of other variables, especially education (e) and children (c'''), were included. Unemployment also carries similar coefficients as it did in Table 15, and, in fact, reaches its highest value in line 6 where Δp and mg are included. These latter two variables are both significant, but only mg has the expected, positive sign. The significant negative sign of Δp is a puzzle.[24]

The control over the fraction of the population that is aged (shown in line 7) had little effect when the variables for the presence of children, female education, and non-labor income were also included. The three latter variables were highly correlated with a_{65}, but none was weakened when a_{65} entered the regression. (A variable that measured the per cent of the population aged 18 to 64 was not significant either.)

A surprising result of Table 18 is the complete failure of the variable for the change in employment to show any effect (see lines 8–9). Even

[23] The employment data stem from the Bureau of Labor Statistics and are available only for 90 of the 100 SMA's in the sample. All other variables are from the 1960 census.

[24] The percentage change in the number of households in the SMA was also tried, and the effect was similar to the population change variable.

when ΔL was entered into the regression before u (its competitor in the model), it showed no significant effect.[25] Although ΔL measures the change in total non-agricultural employment in the area, rather than changes in the female hiring industries alone, both changes are undoubtedly highly correlated. More experimentation with a selection of industries and of different time periods would be informative.

Summary

The tests in this section have consistently rejected the added worker hypothesis and have supported the hypothesis that the net effect of unemployment on the labor force participation of wives is negative. However, the dynamic factors that are at work in affecting labor force participation of secondary workers are inadequately represented in the cross-section model. These lead one to suspect that the magnitude of the effect of unemployment may be overstated, particularly if the responses are projected over a short time span

One interpretation of the negative effect of unemployment is that it supports the idea that the wage variable is more powerful than the income variable on the labor supply of wives as these effects operate in the short run, just as this idea is supported by the long-run rise in work rates of wives. Alternative uses of the non-leisure time of secondary workers like wives make them relatively sensitive to changes in wages and other conditions of employment.

An application of the model to other groups of secondary workers, like teenagers and the aged, support the finding made with data for wives. (See Appendix J for some evidence on this point, and the paper by Bowen and Finegan, cited previously, for a good deal more evidence.) Further, these findings with cross-section data are supported by evidence from the time series.[26] The one group of secondary workers for whom a significant negative effect of unemployment is not found is nonwhite wives. The analysis of the census data for nonwhite married women is taken up in the next section of this chapter. The focus, however, will be on all the basic variables in the model—wages, income, the presence of children, etc.—and not primarily on the unemployment variable.

[25] Employment figures were available in 1949 and 1950 for only 22 of the 77 SMA's in 1950 that were used in Table 11. Trials with this small sample did not reveal any significance of ΔL either.

[26] The several studies using time series data for tests of the effect of unemployment are cited and evaluated by Mincer, "Labor Force Participation and Unemployment: A Review of Recent Evidence."

Regression Results with Nonwhite Married Women Using 1950 Census Data (Table 19)

The analysis of the labor force participation of nonwhite married women is handicapped by data that are inferior to that available for the total population of wives. The necessary labor force and income variables for cities or metropolitan areas are not available for 1940. In 1950 such information is provided for only 29 of the SMA's with 250,000 or more population. The best available earnings measures with these data are median incomes of all (nonwhite) males, y', and all (nonwhite) females, w'. The weakness of w' as a proxy for the "true" concept of the wage rate has already been discussed in connection with the regressions for the total population in 1950 and 1940. No statistics of income from non-wage or salary sources are available for the nonwhite population.

Considering these qualifications, the regressions for nonwhites shown in Table 19 look fairly similar to regressions in Table 11 for the total population in 1950. Compared with the 1950 results, the wage effect is smaller relative to the income effect for nonwhites. It is likely that this partly reflects the weaker wage proxy used, but may also indicate a "real" difference. The latter may be explained with reference to the time series behavior for the two color groups in the years around 1950.

With both wages of females and incomes of husbands rising, the relatively slow increase in participation rates among nonwhite wives implies, *ceteris paribus*, that the negative income effect is relatively stronger than the positive wage effect than with white wives. If we grant that the elasticities of w' and y' are about the same size in absolute value for nonwhite wives, however, then the reconciliation with the time series increase in labor force participation rates depends on the earnings of nonwhite females increasing proportionately more than male earnings. This is the case, as will be brought out in the final comments of this section on the regressions with census aggregates.

Among the supplementary variables, r, standing for a southern SMA, is positive but not consistently significant. The variables representing children, unemployment of nonwhite males, and education are not statistically significant in Table 19, in contrast to the findings for the total population. The signs of u, c, and e, however, are the same in regressions for both the nonwhite and total populations.

The intercept values for nonwhite wives are larger than those in the corresponding regressions for the total population. Higher levels of labor force participation among nonwhite wives leads us to expect these larger intercept values, although with these data this may result from errors in the variables and the consequent flattening of the regression surface. Table 19A shows both a weak wage effect and a large intercept with the total population when w' and y' are used; the participation rate of total wives is the regressor. Compare the regression in Table 19A with line 4 in Table 11, where the regression coefficients for y and w are −0.16 and 1.09, and the intercept is 4.74.

TABLE 19

REGRESSION RESULTS WITH NONWHITE MARRIED WOMEN, 29 SMA'S IN 1950[a]

Line	Form[b]	R^2	Independent Variables						
			Constant	y'	w'	r	c	u	e
1....	A	.55	34.81	−1.48 (.55)	2.88 (.67)	6.89 (3.09)	....	....	....
2....	L	.58	1.09	− .96 (.31)	.84 (.18)	.21 (.09)	....	....	....
3....	A	.58	45.31	−1.39 (.54)	2.92 (.66)	7.85 (3.11)	−.30 (.21)	....	....
4....	L	.61	.99	− .96 (.36)	.73 (.20)	.19 (.12)	....	−.17 (.13)	.46 (.45)
5....	A	.58	45.08	−1.35 (.58)	2.85 (.72)	6.99 (4.58)	−.25 (.28)	−.16 (.63)	....
6....	L	.63	2.20	− .99 (.36)	.79 (.20)	.11 (.06)	−.32 (.31)	−.02 (.15)	.40 (.46)

[a] Dependent variable: labor force participation rate of nonwhite married women, husband present.
[b] A = arithmetic; L = logarithmic.

Definitions of independent variables (see Appendix A for sources, means, and standard deviations)
- y' median income of nonwhite males with income, 1949 (hundreds of dollars)
- w' median income of nonwhite females with income, 1949 (hundreds of dollars)
- r dummy variable for the region of the U.S.: "1" is a southern SMA; "0" otherwise
- c per cent of nonwhite husband-wife families with one or more children under 18 years of age
- u nonwhite male unemployment rate in 1950
- e median years of schooling completed of nonwhite females, 25 years and older

TABLE 19A

EXPERIMENTAL REGRESSION: TOTAL MARRIED WOMEN, 77 SMA'S IN 1950

	R^2	Constant	y'	w'	r
Dependent variable: labor force participation rate of married women, husband present (arithmetic form)......	.36	10.99	.05 (.18)	.77 (.21)	5.13 (1.00)

In one series of regressions with nonwhite data, the median amount of non-labor income received among the total population was added on the chance that it might serve as a proxy for this type of income among nonwhite families. The results were surprising, to put it mildly. The variable for non-labor income, y_n, among the total population had a positive sign with respect to labor force participation rates among nonwhite wives. The coefficient was significant in arithmetic regressions; insignificant in the log form.

Since y_n was also positive and significant (in both arithmetic and log forms) in the regressions with 1960 data for nonwhites, the relation calls for some comment.[27] A frank comment is that I am at a loss to account satisfactorily for this result. Are relatively large receipts of non-labor income among the white population conducive to a favorable job market for nonwhite females? If a high income from non-labor sources indicates a strong demand for the service industry, the answer could well be affirmative. The case is probably strongest with regard to the occupation of domestic service.[28] As a test of this conjecture regressions were run with the following dependent variables: (1) the per cent of the nonwhite female work force in the domestic service occupation in the SMA; and (2) the number of nonwhite domestic servants per 100 persons in the SMA. Non-labor income was one of the independent variables. These tests were of a preliminary nature, and the results were inconclusive. The coefficient of y_n was positive in both regressions but significant in (1) only.

Regression Results with Nonwhite Married Women Using 1960 Census Data (Table 20)

In 1960 there were 66 SMA's (population over 250,000) with labor force data for nonwhite wives, a substantial increase over the 29 observations available for 1950. Another improvement was an alternative wage variable, w'', median earnings for the nonwhite female experienced civilian labor force. The corresponding figure for males, y'', serves as a proxy for the income of the husband. For the total population the simple correlations between y and y'' and w and w'' were .98 and .90 respectively. Finally, the average number of weeks worked for nonwhite females for each SMA could be computed, and from this a weekly wage earnings measure was devised.

The first four lines in Table 20 show that the decline in the wage effect relative to the income effect, noticeable among the total population of wives for 1960 (Table 15), is evident among the nonwhites. Even for the three-variable regression on line 1 the wage coefficient is smaller than the income coefficient. The regional variable remains of lesser importance than for whites. Education and unemployment gain significance in 1960 compared to 1950 and retain their expected signs. Especially noteworthy is the near zero coefficient of c''', the number of children ever born to

[27] The arithmetic coefficients were around 2.0 in both the 1950 and 1960 regressions, and the significant log coefficient in 1960 was about 0.02.

[28] Domestic service is the largest occupational group among nonwhite females (see p. 87). Non-labor income is probably positively related with the dispersion of income in an SMA, and Stigler found the latter measure to be correlated with the number of domestic servants in a labor market. George J. Stigler, *Domestic Servants in the United States*, 1900–1940, Occasional Paper, No. 24 (New York: The National Bureau of Economic Research, 1946).

married women in the SMA.[29] It seems clear from both 1950 and 1960 results that the presence of children has a much weaker effect on participation rates of nonwhite wives than of white wives.[30]

The intercept term for nonwhites in the simplest, three-variable model (lines 1 and 2) is larger than the comparable term in regressions 5 and 6 of Table 15. With the addition of more variables the constant term in the regression of total wives is raised relative to the comparable nonwhite regression. (Compare lines 3 of Table 20 and 4 of Table 15.) It is particularly

TABLE 20

REGRESSION RESULTS WITH NONWHITE MARRIED WOMEN, 66 SMA'S IN 1960[a]

LINE	FORM[b]	R^2	INDEPENDENT VARIABLES							
			Constant	y''	w''	w'''	r	u	e	c'''
1...	L	.45	2.21	−.89 (.17)	.64 (.11)	....	.05 (.03)	....	....	....
2...	A	.42	51.32	−.97 (.22)	1.45 (.27)	....	4.03 (2.55)	....	....	....
3[c]...	L	.51	2.01	−.93 (.20)	.53 (.13)	....	.03 (.03)	−.09 (.07)	.43 (.26)	.01 (.25)
4...	A	.49	47.43	−.97 (.25)	1.12 (.32)	....	1.90 (2.77)	−.55 (.29)	1.53 (1.11)	.00 (.04)
5...	L	.44	2.00	−.93 (.10)	....	.75 (.13)	.07 (.03)	....	....	....
6...	L	.49	2.00	−1.04 (.18)	....	.59 (.11)	.05 (.03)	....	.52 (.24)	....
7...	L	.50	1.98	−.90 (.20)	....	.61 (.14)	.05 (.03)	−.12 (.07)	.32 (.26)	....
8...	L	.50	2.41	−.91 (.20)	....	.57 (.15)	.04 (.03)	−.12 (.07)	.30 (.26)	−.24 (.61)

[a] Dependent variable: labor force participation rate of married women, husband present.

[b] A = arithmetic; L = logarithmic.

[c] Regression 3 is reproduced as the first line in Table 22, and on the second line of Table 22 is a regression that has identically defined variables for the total population. These two regressions provide the most direct comparison of results for the two color groups for 1960.

Definitions of independent variables (see Appendix A for sources, means, and standard deviations)

- y'' median earnings of the nonwhite male civilian labor force, 1959 (in hundreds of dollars)
- w'' median earnings of the nonwhite female civilian labor force, 1959 (in hundreds of dollars)
- w''' median full-year earnings of the nonwhite female civilian labor force (in hundreds of dollars). See Appendix A for full definition.
- r dummy variable for the region of the U.S.: "1" is a southern SMA; "0" otherwise
- u nonwhite male unemployment rate (in per cent)
- e median years of schooling completed of nonwhite females, 25 years and older
- c''' number of children ever born per 1,000 nonwhite women ever married

the variable for children, which has a significantly negative coefficient for the total and essentially a zero coefficient for nonwhites, that raises the constant term for the total.[31]

[29] Among nonwhites it might make a difference if we restricted the children variable to families where the husband is present instead of using c'''—a more loosely defined variable that was chosen simply because it was more accessible. The variable used in the 1950 regressions with nonwhite wives was c, however, the per cent of husband-wife families with one or more children under 18, and this was also insignificant.

[30] The same finding has been made in two other studies: Bancroft, *The American Labor Force*, p. 61, and James N. Morgan, Martin H. David, Wilbur J. Cohen, and Harvey E. Brazier, *Income and Welfare in the United States* (New York: McGraw-Hill, 1962) pp. 110–11.

[31] The situation is basically as follows: Let a be the intercept, and subscripts t and n refer to total and nonwhite populations. First, $m_t = a_t + \ldots + b_t c_t$, so

$$a_t = m_t - \ldots - b_t c_t, \tag{1}$$

The last four regressions in Table 20 use a wage variable, w''', that is closer to the more appropriate full-time earnings figure. The new variable, w''', is the median earnings for the nonwhite female experienced civilian work force (w'') divided by the average weeks worked by nonwhite females who worked. This quotient gives a measure for the average weekly wage, which is then multiplied by 51, the midpoint of the 50–52 weeks bracket that defines full-time workers. There are several changes, none striking, but all in a direction that supports the hypothesis that nonwhite and white behavior are similar. The wage effect is increased proportionately more than is the income effect, and the coefficients and significance levels of the variables for unemployment and region become more similar to those in the regressions with the total population.

Let us conclude this section by calculating the approximations of income and substitution effects for nonwhite wives, using the results for 1950 and 1960. The limitations of the data restrict the estimating procedure of the substitution elasticity, a_3', to equation (5), which uses the husband's income in place of non-labor income for the income elasticity term. Assuming a_2', the cross-elasticity of the husband's wage rate on the wife's labor supply, to be zero, we again have:

$$a_3' = b_2' - (b_1')\left(\frac{W\hat{M}}{Y\hat{Q}}\right) \qquad (5)$$

From line 6 of Table 19 the wage elasticity, b_2', is .79, and the elasticity of the male's (husband's) income, b_1', is $-.99$. The ratio of average female earnings to male earnings, w'/y', is .46. This gives us for 1950:

$$a_3' = 1.25$$

For 1960 we might select from Table 20, .6 as an average wage elasticity and $-.9$ as an income elasticity. The ratio of means, w''/y'', is .64 (from Table 37 in Appendix A). This produces for 1960:

$$a_3' = 1.18$$

The weighting factors, that compensate for changes in $W\hat{M}/Y\hat{Q}$ as W changes, slightly lower our "upper boundary" estimates of the substitution effect. For both 1950 and 1960 the relative change in nonwhite females' earnings across SMA's exceeds the relative change in nonwhite

---

where b_t is negative so that $-b_t c_t$ is positive. Second, $m_n = a_n + \ldots + b_n c_n$ and since $b_n = 0$

$$a_n = m_n - \ldots \qquad (2)$$

Comparing (1) with (2), we observe that a_t is increased as $-b_t$ is large in absolute value, but a_n will not be increased since $b_n = 0$.

males' earnings on the basis of the log regressions: $(d \log w')/(d \log y') = 1.16$ in 1950, and $(d \log w'')/(d \log y'') = 1.25$ in 1960.[32] Multiplying the income elasticity terms by the reciprocals of these log coefficients gives different measures of the substitution elasticity: 1950, $a_3' = 1.18$; and 1960, $a_3' = .97$.

All these estimates are rather close, ranging between 1.18 and 1.25 for 1950 and .97 and 1.18 for 1960. They are also similar to the corresponding values that apply to white wives, which were around 1.35 in 1950 and .85 in 1960.

THE WHITE-NONWHITE DIFFERENTIALS. MORE REGRESSIONS FROM THE 1960 CENSUS (TABLES 21 AND 22) AND SUPPLEMENTARY MATERIALS

The principal issues examined in this section concern the similarities and differences of the same independent variables as they affect participation rates of white and nonwhite wives. Special attention will be given to the question of the higher levels of participation rates by nonwhite wives.

The first model tests whether the larger participation rates for nonwhite wives for each SMA (m_{ni} greater than m_{ti} for the *ith* SMA) can be explained by the differences in the values that the independent variables have for each color group in each individual SMA. Those factors that represent general characteristics of the SMA (like its region, climate, industrial structure, size, etc.) are "held constant" by definition. The model explaining differences within each SMA cannot include the characteristics that are common to both white and nonwhite wives.

The restriction imposed in the specification of this model, equation (3) below, is that all regression coefficients except the intercept term are the same. The derivation is as follows:

$$m_{ni} = a_n + b_1 y_{ni} + b_2 w_{ni} + \ldots \quad (1)$$

$$m_{ti} = a_t + b_1 y_{ti} + b_2 w_{ti} + \ldots \quad (2)$$

Subtracting:

$$(m_{ni} - m_{ti}) = (a_n - a_t) + b_1(y_{ni} - y_{ti}) + b_2(w_{ni} - w_{ti}) + \ldots \quad (3)$$

Our expectation is that the amount by which work rates of nonwhite wives exceeds the rates of white wives will be *less* the closer the incomes of non-

[32] In 1950 the correlation between y' and w' was around .8 for both log and arithmetic values. The arithmetic regression coefficient of w' on y' was 0.50. In 1960 the correlation between w'' and y'' was .83 (arithmetic) and .86 (log), and the arithmetic regression coefficient, 0.56. These results are similar to those for the whites. One notable difference is that increases in white male earnings are matched by the increases in female earnings across the sample of SMA's, but the increases in nonwhite female earnings exceed those of nonwhite male earnings (see the discussion of this point on p. 51).

white husbands are to those of white husbands; that is, we expect b_1 to be negative. Similarly, we expect a greater difference in work rates the less the wages of white wives exceed those of nonwhite wives, so the coefficient on $(w_{ni} - w_{ti})$ is expected to be positive. The regression results are shown below in Table 21 for the logarithmic form of the model.[33]

The income and wage variables behave according to our expectations and appear to satisfy the restriction that the parameters b_{ni} and b_{ti} are equal. The fact that the other variables do not hold up is not surprising given our previous findings for the insignificance of c''', e, and u for the separate regressions with nonwhite data.

TABLE 21

REGRESSION RESULTS OF THE LOGARITHMIC DIFFERENCES OF THE LABOR FORCE PARTICIPATION RATES OF NONWHITE AND TOTAL MARRIED WOMEN IN 1960[a]

R^2	Independent Variables					
	Constant	y''	w''	c'''	e	u
.20.....	.12	−.55 (.22)	.40 (.13)	.10 (.25)	−.03 (.13)	−.04 (.04)
.20.....	.12	−.58 (.17)	.39 (.13)	....	....	−.04 (.04)
.18.....	.10	−.62 (.17)	.41 (.12)	....	....	....

[a] Dependent variable: labor force participation rate of married women, husband present: log of nonwhites minus log of total (log m_n — log m_t).

Definitions of independent variables (see Appendix A for sources, means, and standard deviations)
- y'' log of median income in 1959 of nonwhite males in civilian labor force minus log of median income in 1959 of total males in civilian labor force.
- w'' log of median income in 1959 of nonwhite females in civilian labor force minus log of median income in 1959 of total females in civilian labor force
- c''' log of number of children ever born per 1,000 nonwhite women ever married minus log of number of children ever born per 1,000 total women ever married
- e log of median years of schooling completed of nonwhite females, 25 years and older minus the log of median years of schooling completed of total females, 25 years and older
- u log of nonwhite male unemployment rate minus log of total male unemployment rate

Now look at Table 22. In the first two regressions of this table, the variables are identically defined for both color groups. The intercept terms are shown to be nearly the same for both groups, but this is mainly because of the comparatively large negative coefficient of the children variable for the total population (see pp. 75–76, footnote 31). Indeed, the smaller (negative) income effect for the total wives compared with nonwhite wives and the effect of children are the only important differences in the regressions on lines 1 and 2 for the two color groups.

Thus, a considerable part of the question of why nonwhite wives participate in the labor force more really involves another question: Why does the presence of children not inhibit work by nonwhite wives? It turns

[33] The model underlying the log regression is: $m_n/m_t = a(y''_n/y''_t)^{b_1}(w''_n/w''_t)^{b_2} \ldots$

TABLE 22

Miscellaneous Regression Results with SMA's in 1960

Dependent Variable[a]	Line	Form[b]	R^2	Independent Variables													
				Constant	y	y''	w	w''	w'''	r	c'	c'''	u	e	n	woh	mg
LFPR of nonwhite wives	1	L	.51	2.01	....	−.93 (.20)	.....	.53 (.13)	.....	.03 (.03)	.....	.01 (.25)	−.09 (.07)	.43 (.26)	....	.....	.....
LFPR of total wives	2	L	.46	2.41	....	−.67 (.15)	.....	.42 (.11)	.....	.04 (.03)	.....	−.30 (.15)	−.09 (.03)	.51 (.14)	....	.....	.....
LFPR based on average weeks worked of nonwhite females[c]	3	L	.46	1.68	....	−.96 (.20)	.....	.....	.91 (.14)	.11 (.03)	.....	....	....	....	....	.....	.....
	4	L	.55	3.14	....	−.86 (.22)	.....	.....	.63 (.16)	.05 (.03)	.....	−.45 (.25)	−.18 (.07)	.04 (.28)	....	.....	.....
LFPR of total wives	5	A	.35	15.37	−.27 (.13)	....	.46 (.17)	.....	.....	.94 (1.23)	−10 (11)	....	−.22 (.12)	1.40 (.62)	8.07 (5.70)	.96 (.59)	.04 (.05)
	6	L	.42	1.16	−.40 (.21)	....	.49 (.17)	.....	.....	.03 (.02)	−06 (11)	....	−.16 (.03)	.37 (.22)	−.02 (.02)	.08 (.04)	.04 (.03)
	7	L	.42	1.04	−.46 (.20)	....	.53 (.17)	.....	.....	.034 (.017)	−03 (11)	....	−.15 (.03)	.51 (.19)	−.02 (.02)	.08 (.04)	.....

[a] LFPR stands for "labor force participation rate."

[b] A = arithmetic; L = logarithmic.

[c] LFPR based on average weeks worked is defined as

(LFPR) × (average weeks worked)/52.

The mean is 30.04 and the standard deviation is 5.64.

Definitions of independent variables (see Appendix A for sources, means, and standard deviations)

- y median income for male family heads, spouse present, 1959 (hundreds of dollars)
- y'' median earnings of the male civilian labor force, 1959 (hundreds of dollars)
- w median income of females who worked 50–52 weeks in 1959 (hundreds of dollars)
- w'' median earnings of the female civilian labor force, 1959 (hundreds of dollars)
- w''' median full-time earnings of nonwhite females in the civilian labor force, 1959 (hundreds of dollars). See Appendix A for full definition.
- r dummy variable for the region of the U.S.: "1" is a southern SMA; "0" otherwise
- c' per cent of families with one or more children under six years of age
- c''' number of children ever born per 1,000 women ever married
- u male unemployment rate (in per cent)
- e median years of schooling completed of females, 25 years and older
- n the per cent nonwhite in the SMA
- woh the per cent of husband-wife families without own household
- mg the percent of the population who are in-migrants (i.e. lived in a different county five years ago)

out not to be coincidental, then, that the three following suggested explanations for the higher levels of participation by nonwhite wives are all in part addressed to the question of the difference in the effect of children. The regressions on lines 3–7 of Table 22 will provide some quantitative evidence for these explanations.

The Definition of Labor Supply

Participation rates tell what proportion of a group is *in* the labor force but indicate nothing of the *extent* of participation—that is, the number of hours, days, or weeks worked during the given time period. If we accept hours worked per year (or per lifetime) as the most appropriate definition of the amount of labor supplied, then the use of participation rates overstates the amount of work by nonwhite wives relative to white wives. There is a good deal of evidence that nonwhite women who work are much less likely to have full-time jobs than white women who work (see Appendix D for supporting data). Moreover, the prevalence of part-time work by nonwhite wives helps explain why the presence of children appears to be a less inhibiting factor, since scheduling time for child care is made easier.

The 1960 census data for SMA's gives weeks worked by sex and color, but not by marital status. On the assumption that the average weeks worked by nonwhite females in an SMA bears some fixed relation to the same figure for nonwhite wives, we can use this to compute an alternative measure of labor supply: a participation rate based on weeks worked, which is then used as the dependent variable.[34]

The results, shown in regressions 3 to 4 of Table 22, are interesting in several respects:

(*a*) The coefficient for the wage rate gets larger and the income coefficient becomes smaller, which makes their relative size similar to the case of the total population (see Table 15).

(*b*) The effect of children is negative and is closer to significance than in any other regression for nonwhites. One interpretation of this is that the measure of labor supply that takes account of the variations in *extent* of participation will show a negative effect for the presence of children among nonwhites.

(*c*) The strong significance of the unemployment variable is probably expressing a mechanical relationship—the higher the unemployment rate

[34] The average number of weeks worked by working females is multiplied by the labor force participation rate to give the average weeks worked for all females. This number is divided by 52. The quotient is a participation rate based on the number of weeks worked out of the possible 52 weeks in a year.

in the area, the less the number of weeks worked, and the lower the participation rate based on weeks worked.[35]

Housing Expenditures

Another reason for the higher labor force participation rate among nonwhite wives is suggested by two striking characteristics of their households: the greater incidence of crowding and doubling-up among families and the relatively low quality of the dwellings.[36] These two characteristics are, of course, related, but they involve different empirical evidence in this section.

Joint occupancy of a dwelling unit often would facilitate baby-sitting services and give the mother more latitude in arranging for market work. If, for example, two husband-wife families shared a dwelling unit, then the freeing of one wife for market work would produce a high labor force participation rate of 50 per cent. Crowding, however, has a more ambiguous interpretation. Crowded conditions could indicate that a family occupied a small dwelling unit, and this should lead to more market work. But when the "crowding" represents a large sized family then more homework is probably involved. It is difficult to predict a priori whether a variable for the population density of housing would yield a positive or negative effect.[37]

Within the white and nonwhite populations, conditions of housing would be expected to reflect such factors as tastes and income and would be associated with differential labor force participation rates of wives because of these factors. *Between* the two color groups, however, an exogenous factor may be present that affects housing and indirectly market work by wives; namely, discrimination in the housing market and an associated "tax" on the housing expenditures of nonwhites.

Such a "tax" would carry an income effect inducing more work by the family members, but more important is the price effect inducing a substitution from home goods to market goods. It seems reasonable that homework by the wife is complementary to the quantity and quality of housing

[35] If we accept the findings from Tables 19 and 20 that the effect of unemployment on participation rates is nil, then the interpretation of the coefficient on the weeks-worked rate is as follows: for a 100 per cent increase in the nonwhite male unemployment rate (say from 6 per cent to 12 per cent), the average weeks worked by the employed nonwhite wife would decline by 18 per cent (line 4 of Table 22). This would amount to a decline of about 6½ weeks from an average of 36 weeks.

[36] In Appendix G this and other statements made in the following several paragraphs are examined further and given supporting evidence.

[37] A variable giving the per cent of households with 1.01 or more persons per room was tried in several regressions, and it was insignificantly different from zero.

purchased. Evidence for the existence of a discrimination tax is quite meager, however, and I have relegated both the theoretical case for discrimination and the empirical evidence to Appendix G.

In Table 22 one test of whether doubling-up contributes to greater labor force participation by the wife is shown. As a proxy for this condition regressions 5 to 7 include the variable, *woh*, the per cent of husband-wife families who are without their own household. The per cent of nonwhites in the SMA is, of course, held constant. Also included in the regressions is the per cent of the population who are in-migrants, *mg*, to guard against *woh* acting as its proxy.

The coefficient of *woh* is positive and significant in the regressions shown, where c', the per cent of families with children under 6 years of age is included. In regressions without c' (not shown) *woh* was positive but not significant. Perhaps *woh* alone acts as a proxy both for doubling-up and for the presence of young children of recent marriages. The latter's negative effect would pull down the former's positive effect.

The relative prevalence of doubling-up among nonwhite families may not be a trivial influence in explaining the higher levels of participation among nonwhites. The average rates of *woh* are 4.5 per cent for nonwhites and 2.1 per cent for the total. Begging the question of what determines the doubling-up (discrimination?), but noting that we do control for income as well as other variables in the regression, the coefficient of 0.08 on *woh* in log form says that for the 100 per cent increase in *woh* (nonwhites over whites) we expect an 8 per cent increase in labor force participation rates. This would account for 2 to 3 of the 10 percentage points in the differences by color. The fact that *woh* is insignificant in some of the regressions, however, casts doubt on the evidence and the interpretations I have drawn.

Family Instability

A third explanation for the high rates of labor force participation by nonwhite wives is the prevalence of marital instability of Negro families. Excluding single women who have never married, 41 per cent of nonwhite females 14 years old and over were either separated (comprising 23 per cent) or widowed or divorced in March, 1959. In the similar age group of white females 22 per cent fell into these three categories, and only 4 per cent were separated.[38] Given the relatively high probability that the Negro wife will be without her husband during part of her married life, it seems likely that she would maintain closer ties to the labor force while

[38] "The Economic Situation of Negroes in the United States," U.S. Department of Labor, Bulletin S-3, October, 1960, p. 2 (hereafter cited as: "The Economic Situation of Negroes").

married.[39] And keeping a job is even more likely if payments for child-support and alimony are uncommon so that the major burden of providing for dependents falls on the wife. These conditions constitute another reason why the presence of children is less deterring to work by nonwhite wives. Furthermore, the statistics on marital instability and the interpretation given to them offer some empirical content to the sociological hypothesis that Negro wives work more because of their matriarchal family structure.[40]

To test the marital instability hypothesis rigorously, one would want a control group with all relevant characteristics the same as Negroes, except for that of marital instability. This is not feasible and, instead, we can look for differential labor force behavior among those wives in the white population who have remarried or separated. If we assume that they will exhibit patterns of labor force participation like groups who are prone to marital instability, we can test whether the net effect on work of their record of instability is positive. I use survey data for this test, and the results presented in the second part of this chapter do conform to this stated expectation.

General Comments on the Regression Results of the Census Aggregates

An Over-all Appraisal

Two general assessments of the regression results for the three census years are that they have considerable internal consistency and that they are compatible with the customary considerations of economic theory.[41] We have found that the wage effect, and implicitly the substitution effect, was consistently positive and the effect of income consistently negative for samples of both total and nonwhite wives. The effect of the presence

[39] As in the case of the effects of housing expenditures on participation, differences in marital stability *among* white and nonwhite wives may largely reflect tastes (or "personality") differences. And, indeed, tastes for market work and against homework by a wife may lead to a marital break-up. *Between* whites and Negroes, however, the difference in marital instability probably reflects broader cultural factors that impinge upon the individual.

[40] See, E. Franklin Frazier, *The Negro in the United States* (rev. ed.; New York: Macmillan, 1957), pp. 306–33 and 623–37 and the references cited. Frazier emphasizes the slave system as providing the roots for a matriarchal family structure among Negroes.

[41] The favorable verdict, in turn, depends on the validity of the techniques of measurement; in this case, least-squares estimates of single equation models. One effort to take account of simultaneity in the system did not result in any changes of these signs, but other aspects of the model were unsatisfactory. The simultaneous system is presented in Appendix H.

of children was significantly negative for total wives but not for nonwhite wives.

In the case of the effect of unemployment on wives' labor force participation rates, where theoretical considerations indicated both a positive and a negative influence, a definite answer has emerged. The regression coefficient of the male unemployment rate was persistently negative for total wives, although not significantly so for nonwhite wives. This leads to a rejection of the "added worker hypothesis" with regard to wives, numerically the most important group of secondary workers, and Appendix J contains evidence that unemployment has a net deterrence on participation rates among the other groups of secondary workers. The low labor force rates of wives in the period from 1930–1940 compared with 1940–1960 may be partly attributable to the high levels of unemployment in the earlier period.

The signs of the elasticities of wages and income were given special attention because of their relevance to the time series of labor force participation of wives. If we find that the wage elasticity is larger than the income elasticity, an important part of the explanation of the time series is made.[42] This finding holds, unambiguously, only for data of 1950 when the wage effect exceeded the income effect in all regressions. In 1940 and 1960 this is true only when the supplementary variables for children and education are omitted from the regressions.

A rationalization for the diminishment of the wage effect when variables for education and children are included is that the latter two act, in part, as proxies for the underlying wage effect. It is difficult to avoid some conjecture in making these arguments, even though empirical evidence for these interpretations exist. Several cross-section studies have shown that the number of children has a strong inverse relation to the wife's potential market earnings.[43] If this is true a variable representing the presence of children will serve partly as a proxy for a wage effect as long as the selected empirical wage rate does not fully reflect the "true" concept.

[42] This implies a belief, which I hold, that the effects of wages and income that show up in cross-sections also apply in a very similar way to the time series, given some allowance or control for transitory components.

[43] See Jacob Mincer, "Market Prices, Opportunity Costs, and Income Effect," in *Measurement in Economics* (Stanford: Stanford University Press, 1963), pp. 67–82. My own preliminary trials using regressions with the 1960 data show a strong negative relation between a fertility variable, c''', and a female wage rate in a multiple regression for both nonwhites and the total. (Education, husbands' income, and wives' labor force participation rates were included along with the female wage rate as independent variables.) See also the negative correlations between wives' average earnings and average fertility rate reported in Ronald Freedman and Doris P. Slesinger, "Fertility Differentials for the Indigenous Non-Farm Population of the United States," *Population Studies* (November, 1961), p. 161.

The assertion that education partly reflects a wage effect, by acting as a proxy for non-pecuniary returns for market work, probably has more immediate intuitive appeal. On the other hand education may, in a cross-section sample, represent tastes for market work. Evidence on the extent to which either of these propositions is true would be difficult to obtain. One test of the first would be whether there is a positive relation between the educational attainment of female workers and the amount of fringe benefits they receive, since these are not included in the measure of median earnings I have used. As a test of the hypothesis regarding tastes, high school girls might be asked their attitudes toward marriage and/or work; then their work histories and years of school completed could be ascertained later in life.

The interpretation of the effects of both the presence of children and of the educational attainment of wives, however, differs in important respects depending on whether cross-sections or time series are being analyzed. In the long run of decades the reduction in the fertility rate has been attributable in large part to advances in birth control knowledge and techniques and their spread among all segments of the adult population. In cross-sections the variation in birth control knowledge is much less (although not zero) than it is in the time series. The interpretation that low fertility rates of a group of wives is an important proxy for their high earnings abilities is more tenable in cross-sections than it could be in the time series. In appraising the influence of education over time, I would argue that advances in education were more a result of rises in income than changes in tastes. These advances, with coincident vocational training aspects, have perhaps brought about increases in female wages (including non-pecuniary aspects) that are not fully represented by the money wage changes.

Summary Comments on the White-Nonwhite Differential

Comparisons between the regression results for the total and nonwhite populations that involved two important differences, the children variable and the intercept term, have already been discussed. The effects of the variables for income and wages are generally similar between the two groups as shown, in particular, by Tables 21 and 22—similar, but not identical.

In the regressions for 1950 and 1960 for the total and nonwhite groups, a persistent difference was the lower size of the wage elasticity relative to the income elasticity for nonwhites. Note, however, that this difference is consistent with the time series changes in labor force participation rates for the two color groups. The increase in work rates for white wives has been greater than for nonwhites (see Table 10), as a relatively large wage effect implies since this effect is positive. Furthermore, the near equality (in absolute value) of the wage and income elasticities for nonwhite wives is consistent with the rise in participation rates in recent years, since the percentage increase in nonwhite female earnings has exceeded that of nonwhite male earnings. Table 23 shows these changes for both whites and nonwhites over a time span, 1939 to 1957, appropriate to this discussion.

For both color groups we can apply the 1950 arithmetic regression coefficients (from lines 6 of Table 11 and 1 of Table 19) to the dollar changes in wage and salary incomes (adjusted for price changes). This gives a "predicted change" that can be compared to the actual change in labor

TABLE 23

PERCENTAGE INCREASE IN MEDIAN WAGE AND SALARY INCOMES OF YEAR-ROUND, FULL-TIME WORKERS BY SEX AND COLOR: 1939–57 (UNADJUSTED FOR PRICE CHANGES)

	White	Nonwhite
Male	250	390
Female	260	470 410 (adjusted measure)[a]

Source: "The Economic Situation of Negroes in the United States," U.S. Department of Labor, Bulletin S-3 (October, 1960), p. 15.

[a] See Appendix E for the adjustment that takes into account the decline in proportion of nonwhite females in domestic service, where income-in-kind is important.

force rates. The regional dummy variable was omitted since accounting for the population shifts from South to North would scarcely change the results. This is summarized in the table below (see Appendix E for the computations).

The comparison is a rough illustration of the relative wage and income effects over the time span for which regression results were reported in this section. Selecting coefficients from 1950 instead of 1940 or 1960 is natural for the period 1939–1957, but we should not overlook the fact that these coefficients are the "best" ones to match "actual" and "predicted" changes. Furthermore, the importance (or significance) of other variables in the regression models for cross-sections very much complicates a simple application of coefficients for W and Y only to time series data.

If we accept the agreement between the regression results and time series experience, the question of *why* the coefficients and the time series experience differ for white and nonwhite wives remains open. One explanation of the slower rate of increase in work by nonwhite wives is suggested by a characteristic of the occupational distributions; namely the concentration of nonwhites in domestic service. The per cent of nonwhite working women in this occupation was 60 in 1940, 42 in 1950, and 37 in 1960.[44] What happens to domestic service will have an important effect on the labor force behavior of nonwhite females. (You could turn this statement around, of course, but I am going to argue below that changes with regard to the occupation are "causal.")

The per cent of the labor force in domestic service has declined during this century, although recently (1950-1960) this per cent has remained fairly constant. The sharpest decrease occurred between 1940 and 1950,[45]

TABLE 24

CHANGES IN LABOR FORCE PARTICIPATION RATES, 1939–57: PREDICTED AND ACTUAL[a]

	Actual Change, Per Cent	Predicted Change, Per Cent
White wives	15	10
Nonwhite wives		
Using unadjusted earnings	10	7
Using adjusted earnings[b]	10	5.6

[a] See Appendix E for the method of computation for this table.

[b] See Table 23 for adjusted earnings change and Appendix E for the method of computation.

when the work rates of white wives increased much more rapidly than those of nonwhite wives. Any contended causal relation stemming from the occupational change to the work rates of nonwhite wives raises the question: What forces brought about this over-all decline in domestic service?

Home goods may be expected to have a low income elasticity, but this would appear to be offset by the observed high income elasticity for domestic servants coupled with the secular trend toward more market work by wives.[46] The income elasticities from cross-sections, however, as Mincer has demonstrated, are biased upward by a built-in substitution

[44] For 1940 and 1950 see George J. Stigler, *Trends in Employment in the Service Industry* (Princeton: Princeton University Press, 1956), p. 101; for 1960 see Bureau of Labor Statistics "The Economic Situation of Negroes," p. 13.

[45] Stigler, *Trends in Employment in the Service Industry*, p. 7.

[46] Stigler found income elasticities of approximately 2 from cross-sections for three periods between 1919 and 1941. *Ibid.*, p. 27.

effect: the higher the family's income status the more likely the wife could earn a market wage that encourages a substitution of hired domestic service for self service.[47] Given equal rises in wages of both domestic help and other female jobs, this substitution effect would not operate in the time series.

The apparent rise in wages paid to domestic service relative to other jobs[48] implies that the reason for the decline in numbers stems from the supply side. Domestic service is universally looked upon as unattractive work, and it is likely that its labor supply would have a negative income elasticity. This appears to have been the pattern among foreign-born whites and their children. As Stigler commented:

> A striking illustration of the strength of the aversion to domestic service is that children of immigrants enter domestic service in the same proportion as native white women, although their parents enter in twice the proportion.[49]

The leftward shifts in supply over time on this account, coupled with a fairly high price elasticity of the demand for domestic servants, may well have operated to diminish the numbers in this occupation with the outflow going into other jobs and out of the labor force. In turn, the decline in labor force rates by Negro females (or the slow increase by Negro wives) would be related to the special importance this occupation has among them.[50]

Again, we can point to the foreign-born white females who were heavily concentrated in domestic service at the beginning of this century.[51] The time series behavior of foreign-born white females is more similar to that of nonwhite females than to native whites. Relatively high levels of participation were characteristic of both groups during the time when they were most heavily concentrated in domestic service. And from that time the work rates of both groups declined, or increased less rapidly, compared to native white females.[52] Of course, a proof by analogy is not a

[47] Mincer, "Market Prices, Opportunity Costs, and Income Effects," *op. cit.*, p. 75. Mincer estimates that the income effect is biased upward by "more than 50 per cent."

[48] Stigler, *Trends in Employment in the Service Industry*, pp. 94 and 101.

[49] Stigler, *Domestic Servants in the United States*, 1900–1940, pp. 6–7.

[50] Gertrude Bancroft makes this point in perhaps clearer terms. Speaking of the sharp decline in domestic service and of the greater decline in labor force rates for nonwhite females in the South than the North, she states: "The lack of job opportunities in the South in the more attractive, higher paying occupations may well have been the reason why Negro women chose to withdraw from the labor force or to remain at home when family incomes permitted a choice." Bancroft, *op. cit.*, p. 86.

[51] Stigler, *Domestic Servants in the United States*, 1900–1940, p. 7.

[52] Clarence Long, *The Labor Force under Changing Income and Employment*, National Bureau of Economic Research (Princeton: Princeton University Press, 1958), p. 295.

proof; the similarities between the foreign-born and nonwhite females are only suggestive.

REGRESSION RESULTS FOR CROSS-SECTION DISAGGREGATED DATA

The Growth of American Families Survey

The first body of disaggregated data examined is the 1955 nation-wide survey of wives made by the Scripps Population Foundation. The survey, called the Growth of American Families (GAF) study, consisted of a clustered sample of 2,713 white wives who were between the ages of 18 and 39 and living with their husbands.[53] I excluded farm residents (around 300) and the cases where important data were "not ascertained" (around 160).[54]

This survey was used by Sobol for the study discussed in chapter 2. In both her unpublished dissertation and the article based on this research,[55] Dr. Sobol discusses the degree to which clustering violates the assumption of independence among the observations and introduces biases into the significance tests used in regression analysis. She noted in her article that "for this sample, true standard errors were quite similar to simple random errors," for the sample statistics investigated.[56]

Three sets of regressions were computed with these data: (1) using grouped observations, (2) using the current labor force status of the wife with disaggregated data, and (3) using a measure of years worked by the wife, also with disaggregated data.

Aggregative Regressions

The basis for grouping the observations was the particular geographic area (city or county) in which the wives resided—their "sampling cluster points." Means were computed and the regressions fitted were similar in form to those made with SMA's for the decennial censuses. Forty-five of the original 66 cluster points had 20 or more observations (after I made the exclusions noted above), and these 45 areas were the basis for the regressions shown in Table 25. The labor force participation rate and the

[53] The GAF study is fully described in R. Freedman, P. K. Whelpton, and A. A. Campbell, *Family Planning, Sterility, and Population Growth* (New York: McGraw-Hill, 1959). I am indebted to Freedman for his permission to use the survey data and for his and Doris Slesinger's assistance in acquiring the coded punch cards. They are, of course, in no way responsible for the way in which I used these data.

[54] The "not ascertained" cases had been excluded by Ronald Freedman from some of his analyses, and were judged by him not to be distinctly concentrated in any particular category (from a letter sent to me by Freedman).

[55] In Ivan Nye and Lois W. Hoffman, *The Employed Mother in America* (Chicago: Rand McNally, 1963).

[56] *Ibid.*, p. 43.

unemployment rate apply to the time of the survey (1955). Family income and the earnings of the wife refer to the year preceding, 1954, and they may be considered predetermined variables.

Not listed in this table are the regressions in which the following variables were shown to be insignificant: region, industrial structure, number

TABLE 25

REGRESSION RESULTS WITH 45 AREA AGGREGATIONS OF GROWTH OF AMERICAN FAMILIES DATA

DEPENDENT VARIABLE	FORM[a]	R^2	INDEPENDENT VARIABLES: Family Income Minus Wife's Earnings ($00, Mean $46.23)	Earnings of Employed Wives ($00, Mean $5.99)	Area Unemployment Rate (%, Mean 4.17)	Sq. Root of Number of Area Observations[c] (Mean of $n_i = 42$)
LFPR;[b] arithmetic mean, 25.6	A	.47	−0.45 (.13)	2.39 (.40)	−0.36 (.26)	
	L	.38	−0.68 (.25)	0.44 (.09)	−0.04 (.05)	
	A	.45	−0.37 (.12)	2.25 (.40)		
	L	.37	−0.60 (.23)	0.42 (.09)		
LFPR adjusted;[c] arithmetic mean 22.6	A	.55	−0.46 (.11)	2.40 (.35)	−0.41 (.22)	
	L	.50	−0.84 (.24)	0.55 (.09)	−0.08 (.05)	
	A	.51	−0.36 (.10)	2.24 (.35)		
	L	.47	−0.67 (.22)	0.50 (.09)		
Weighted, adjusted LFPR[d]	A	.73	−0.42 (.12)	2.32 (.36)	−0.48 (.23)	29.13 (8.01)
	A	.70	−0.34 (.12)	2.16 (.36)		25.91 (8.15)

[a] A = arithmetic; L = logarithmic.

[b] LFPR = labor force participation rate: 1 if in the labor force; 0 if not in.

[c] Adjusted LFPR: 1 if full-time working wife, ½ if part-time or unemployed, 0 if not in the labor force.

[d] Weighted adjusted LFPR: the model adopted was: $\sqrt{n_i}m = \sqrt{n_i}a + \sqrt{n_i}b_1x_1 + \sqrt{n_i}b_2x_2 + \ldots$ where n_i is the number of observations in the ith area. This guarded against the problem of a non-constant variance across areas, each presumed to be σ^2/n_i.

of children per family, per cent of families with children under 6 years old, wives' education, and husbands' occupational socioeconomic score.[57] The signs of these variables were all "correct," but the lack of significance of some, particularly the children variables, was unexpected. The coefficients of the "economic" variables that appear in Table 25, however, are not much different from the census regressions for SMA's.

Family income has a stronger effect and wives' earnings a weaker ef-

[57] For a definition of the occupational score see the article by O. Dudley Duncan in Albert Reiss, Jr., *Occupation and Social Status* (New York: The Free Press, 1961), pp. 109–38.

fect than in the SMA regressions for 1950, but the coefficients are remarkably similar to those computed with the 1960 SMA data. We have reason to expect, however, that the wage effect would be low (relative to the income effect) with this set of data. The GAF sample is restricted to wives aged 18–39. This age group would have relatively large numbers of young children present. The discussion of the theoretical underpinnings of the model pointed out that where young children are present, the income effect may well be stronger relative to the wage effect.[58] Mincer offered evidence for this point in his study,[59] and the regressions I present below with disaggregated GAF data support this interpretation.[60] Also, an earnings figure for wives that was closer in concept to a wage rate, like weekly earnings, would have been preferable to the annual earnings measure used and would probably have yielded a stronger effect. The unemployment rate is significant in two regressions of Table 25, but the small number of observations makes the calculated rate a doubtful representation of the actual unemployment rate in the area.

Disaggregated Regressions with the Current Labor Force Status of the Wife as the Dependent Variable

Labor force status at a moment-in-time is measured as a dichotomous variable, taking the value of 1 if in the labor force, 0 otherwise. With this as a dependent variable, the regression model is called a "linear probability function." The coefficients and values of the independent variables determine the probability that a wife (with the given characteristics) will be in the labor force.

The concept of labor supply used with the disaggregated data in this section is analogous to the concept for the city and SMA aggregates used previously in this chapter. Both are probability distributions of the binomial variable defined as: 1 if the wife is in the labor force, 0 if the wife is not in the labor force. Summing over all wives in the disaggregated data gives us the proportion of wives in the labor force, which is precisely the labor force participation rate we used with the aggregated data. The mean probability that a wife from the GAF sample was in the labor force at the time of the survey was .266, so about 27 per cent of the wives in the sample were working.

[58] To review this point: market work is not a good substitute for the homework of a mother of young children, and this implies that the market labor supply curve of the mother would be inelastic with respect to the wage. Further, although a low family income might impel the mother to work, moderate increases in income would induce her to leave the labor force and remain at home.

[59] Mincer, "The Labor Force Participation of Married Women," pp. 67–68, and p. 78.

[60] This point will be brought out in comparing Table 27 with Table 26.

The analogy between the regression analysis of the aggregated and disaggregated data extends to the interpretation of the independent variables. We use the regression with disaggregated data to predict the probability that a wife will be in or out of the labor force, given the economic and social characteristics of the wife and her family. With aggregated data we predict the proportion of wives who will be in the labor force given the (typical) values for income, education, etc.

There are a few conceptual statistical problems in the use of dichotomous variables as regressors in least-squares estimation methods, and alternative approaches are employed in this section.[61] One innovation is shown in Table 26. The dependent variable in the regressions takes the value 1, if the wife is a full-time worker, $\frac{1}{2}$ if a part-time worker or unemployed, and 0 if not in the labor force.[62] By this definition the mean probability is .232.

There are two main innovations in the selection of independent variables in Table 26. The first is the construction of a variable other than education to get a measure of the substitution (wage) effect for all wives in the sample. To this end a "potential earnings capacity" was defined for each wife using the survey data on—in order of priority—her current occupation, most recent occupation since marriage, her occupation before marriage, or her educational attainment. Median earnings for these detailed occupational (or educational) groups were obtained from the 1950 census, and these figures were assigned to each wife according to her classification.[63]

The second innovation involves the construction of a measure of the transitory component of income that does not rely exclusively on the unemployment experience of the head of the household. A proxy for the permanent income of the husband, called "predicted income" in the

[61] See Goldberger, *Econometric Theory* (New York: John Wiley and Sons, 1964), pp. 248–55 for a discussion of this problem and for a number of ways of handling it.

[62] Attaching less weight to part-time workers seems reasonable a priori, and the empirical results support this strategy. We have seen in Table 25 a higher R^2 in the regression with the 1, $\frac{1}{2}$, 0 values. Using disaggregated data, regressions were computed (not shown) with a straight 1–0 assignment for the dependent variable, and these yielded a lower R^2, (although nearly the same values for coefficients) than those in Table 26. When separate regressions were computed for only those wives who were in the labor force the differential behavior of full- and part-time workers was also borne out. This point is discussed below in connection with Table 28.

[63] The occupational data were quite detailed, designating nurses, typists, teachers, etc. Only 15 per cent listed no occupation and for this group the education of the wife permitted an assignment of earnings capacity. Again, a measure of median earnings for *full-time* workers in each of the given occupations would have been preferable, but this was not available. Also, the earnings in 1950 are five years prior to the GAF survey, but this is probably not a serious shortcoming. The salary ranking of occupations probably changed very little, although the figures will be somewhat lower than for 1955.

GAF data, was substracted from the reported, current income of the family (not including the wife's earnings), and this difference, positive or negative, was entered as an independent variable. The "predicted income" of the husband is an income figure determined by a multiple regression using the husband's education, age, region, and socioeconomic occupational score.[64]

The results of Table 27 generally support the main lines of argument advanced in this study:

(*a*) The wife's wage variable, "earnings capacity," is positive, significant, and shows up stronger than either the husband's predicted income (line 2) or family income (line 3). The interpretation of the regression coefficients in Table 26 may be illustrated with these variables. For each $100 increase in the wife's earnings capacity, the probability that she will be in the labor force increases by between .0102 and .0134. Thus given a $100 increase in the earnings abilities of all wives we would expect the labor force participation rate to increase by 1.0 to 1.3 percentage points. For each $100 increase in the predicted income of the husband, the probability that a wife will be in the labor force decreases by .0035 to .0040.

The values from the regressions with SMA data were similar if allowance is made for the scaling differences. The elasticities at the mean of the wife's earnings are 0.96 and 0.73 in regressions I and IV, and the elasticity for predicted income is −0.69 in I and −0.47 for current family income in IV. These values are similar to the census aggregate elasticities.

(*b*) The coefficient of the transitory income component (line 4) is negative and significant but smaller in absolute value than the coefficient of the "permanent" or ("predicted") income component. Recall that Mincer had found that the transitory component was larger in the research he conducted (see pages 28–31). His finding may have been the result of defining transitory income as the loss in income stemming from unemployment of the head. The concept defined in this way will include a negative cross-substitution effect—i.e., the husband's availability for homework—in addition to the negative income effect.

There is a good chance that the relative strengths of the two income concepts may hinge on the particular definitions and measures adopted. My results reflect only one approach to the problem of measuring permanent and transitory components. There may well be a lot of errors of measurement caught in the transitory component I devised, since it is a residual that remains after subtracting a tightly measured concept of income from the reported figure.

(*c*) The importance of the demographic variables, revealed by lines

[64] The predicted income variable was developed by Freedman and his associates and was included in the GAF data I received.

TABLE 26

Regression Results for Current Labor Force Status: Disaggregated Data from the Growth of American Families Survey[a]

Independent Variable	Units of Measure	Means	Regression (Coefficients × 100) (Each Column Shows a Multiple Regression)			
			I.	II.[b]	III.[c]	IV.[d]
(1) Wife's earnings capacity.........	$00	16.56	13.4 (2.0) 0.96[e]	12.0 (1.9)	10.9 (2.0)	10.2 (2.0) 0.73[e]
(2) Predicted husband's income....	$00	45.96	− 3.5 (.8) − 0.69[e]	− 3.7 (.8)	− 4.0 (.9)	....
(3) Family income (not including wife's earnings)...	$00	47.38	....	....	....	− 2.3 (.4) − 0.47[e]
(4) Transitory family income: variable (3) minus (2).....	$00	1.42	− 2.4 (.4)	− 1.9 (.4)	− 2.0 (.4)	....
(5) Children under 6 years of age......	Dummy, 1 if yes	0.63	....	−256.9 (19.0)	−265.7 (20.3)	−263.5 (20.3)
(6) Number of children (linear)......	....	1.92	....	−103.3 (15.1)	−110.0 (15.7)	−111.7 (15.7)
(7) Number of children (squared)....	....	5.57	....	12.8 (2.5)	14.5 (2.5)	14.8 (1.6)
(8) Age of wife, 22–29.	Dummy, 1 if yes	0.36	....	....	75.4 (32.9)	68.9 (32.8)
(9) Age of wife, 30–39.	Dummy, 1 if yes	0.57	....	....	45.6 (34.7)	27.8 (33.6)
(10) Education of wife (linear)..........	Years	11.32	....	....	48.0 (17.2)	47.4 (17.2)
(11) Education of wife (squared)........	Years	133.6	....	....	− 1.8 (.8)	− 1.9 (.8)
(12) Income trend, up and down........	Dummy, 1 if yes	0.47	....	....	129.2 (50.4))	128.9 (50.6)
(13) Income trend, up..	Dummy, 1 if yes	0.50	....	....	87.6 (50.6)	85.8 (50.8)
R^2, corrected for degrees of freedom.....	....	......	.033	.202	.211	.208

[a] Dependent variable: current labor force status (1 = full-time workers, ½ = part-time, 0 = not in labor force) of 2,035 wives, white, age 18–39, nonfarm residents not currently pregnant.

Mean value of the dependent variable, the proportion of wives in the labor force is .232.

Mean value of labor force participation rate (with dependent variable defined as above) = 23.2.

[b] The interpretation of "number of children" and "number of children, squared" may be illustrated by regression II. The technique used is to take the first partial derivative of M with respect to C, yielding a first order term for C that is solved for when the first derivative is set equal to zero. We have:

$M = -103.3\ C + 12.8\ C^2 +$ other variables. Therefore, $\partial M/\partial C = -103.3 + 25.6\ C$. Thus, $C = 4$ when $\partial M/\partial C = 0$. Note: $\partial^2 M/\partial C^2 > 0$, so $C = 4$ is a minimum.

Thus, the probability that the wife will work decreases with the number of children to the minimum of about 4 and then rises, holding the presence or absence of children under age 6 constant.

[c] The interpretation of "education" and "education, squared" is shown by regression III. The probability that the wife will work increases with her years of education up to a maximum at 13.3 years and then declines. See technical note to footnote [a] above.

[d] In regression IV unemployment of the husband and urban residence were included but were insignificantly different from zero.

[e] Elasticities at the mean.

5 to 9, is characteristic of regressions with disaggregated data, as was shown in the studies reviewed in chapter 2. One non-obvious result is the positive sign on the variable for the square of the number of children (see footnote *b*, Table 26). Given the presence or absence of children under 6 years of age, the relation between wife's work and number of children is negative over most of the range of the independent variable, reaches a minimum at about four children, and becomes positive from that point. This positive effect of the presence of four or more children may indicate that the oldest children are capable of performing homework.

(*d*) Education (linearly) and its squared term are both significant, even though the major source of the "wage effect" is the "potential earnings" variable. Education shows the expected positive relation to wife's work, reaching a maximum level of about 13 years of schooling.

(*e*) The two variables for income history are difficult to interpret. The trends (up, down, or up-and-down) refer to family income, and it may be that they reflect work by the wife more than they affect her labor force experience. The significant positive effect of an unstable income trend was expected, however. The upward trend—here shown positive but insignificant—was expected to be negative for the same reason that family income itself is expected to have a negative effect.

(*f*) A number of variables tried (regressions not shown) were found to be insignificant. These are listed below.

	Variable	Indicating the Effect of:	Expected Sign
i.	Urban residence	Better employment opportunities	Positive
ii.	Unemployment of husband	Transitory income loss and husband at home	Positive
iii.	Parents living in	Homework substitutes	Positive
iv.	Other adults living in	Market work substitutes	Negative
v.	Owning a house	Tastes for homework	Negative
vi.	Remarried or separated	Marital instability	Positive

Upon reflection, it is dubious whether variables iii and iv should be expected to reflect faithfully the effects listed, since one can easily imagine parents who are ill and need attention, and numerous other such situations.

Supplementary Regressions of Current Labor Force Status

A separate series of regressions were made on those wives who had one or more children under 6 years of age. Two equations are shown in Table 27.

The elasticities for the wife's earnings capacity and for the husband's predicted income in regression I may be compared with the values from regression I in Table 26, which were 0.96 and −0.69 respectively. In Table 27 the elasticities are 0.84 for the wife's earnings capacity and −0.90 for the husband's predicted income. The comparison reveals the expected tendency for the income effect to be slightly larger, the wage effect slightly

TABLE 27

REGRESSION RESULTS FOR CURRENT LABOR FORCE STATUS OF WIVES WHO HAVE ONE OR MORE CHILDREN UNDER 6 YEARS OF AGE: GAF DISAGGREGATED DATA[a]

	Independent Variables (Coefficients ×100)							
	Constant	Wife's Earnings Capacity	Husband's Predicted Income	Husband's Transitory Income	Children, Number	Children, Number Squared	Age, 22–29 (Dummy, 1 if yes)	Age, 30–39 (Dummy, 1 if yes)
Means[b]		$16.53	$45.12	$2.04	2.34	7.16	.450	.471
Regression I[c]	124.9 (39.2)	5.83 (1.86) 0.84[e]	−2.29 (0.79) −0.90[e]	−1.39 (0.44)	......	......	......	......
Regression II[d]	151.9 (49.5)	4.35 (1.92) 0.62[d]	−2.27 (0.86) −0.89[d]	−1.39 (0.44)	−42.2 (19.3)	3.21 (2.75)	80.6 (33.1)	76.8 (35.4)

[a] Dependent variable: current labor force status (1 = full-time workers, ½ = part-time, 0 = not in labor force) for 1,286 wives, non-farm residents, and not currently pregnant, but who have one or more children under 6 years of age.

[b] Mean labor force participation rate of this sample of wives was 11.5. (Alternatively, the mean probability that a wife would be in the labor force is .115.)

[c] R^2 corrected for degrees of freedom is .014.

[d] R^2 corrected for degrees of freedom is .022.

[e] Elasticities at the mean.

smaller, when young children are present. The effect of children is negative over almost the entire range, reaching a minimum at 6.5 children. (The minimum point was reached at 4 children in Table 26). It is likely that among these young mothers even the oldest among the fourth and fifth children are still too young to be good substitutes in homework. The implied negative coefficient of the omitted 18–21 age group probably reflects the presence of very young children (under 3 years of age). The other variables listed in Table 26 were insignificant when included in the regressions in Table 27.

Another check on the regression model being used and on the distinction made between full and part-time workers is given below in a regression with only those wives in the GAF sample who were in the labor force. This model determines the probability that a wife works full-time, given that she is in the labor force. Table 28 shows that the variables that determine being in or out of the labor force are similarly effective in determining extent of participation.

TABLE 28

REGRESSION RESULTS OF EXTENT OF CURRENT LABOR FORCE PARTICIPATION OF WIVES WHO WERE IN THE LABOR FORCE: GAF DISAGGREGATED DATA[a]

	Independent Variables (Coefficients × 100)						
	Constant	Wife's Earnings Capacity	Husband's Predicted Income	Husband's Transitory Income	Children under 6 Years of Age (1 if yes)	Children, Number	Children, Number Squared
Means[b]	....	$17.28	$45.43	−$1.98	0.34	1.31	3.32
Regression I[d]	84.76 (9.45)	2.27 (0.43) 0.53[c]	− 0.80 (0.18) − 0.48[c]	− 0.19 (0.10)	−14.32 (4.25)	−11.42 (3.90)	1.89 (0.94)

[a] Dependent variable: current labor force participation: (full-time worker = 1, part-time or unemployed worker = 0) for 541 wives who were in the labor force.

[b] The mean of the dependent variable, the proportion of wives who were full-time workers, was 0.74. This refers to wives who were working at a full-time job at the time of the survey but does not mean that they worked the whole year.

[c] Elasticities at the mean.

[d] R^2 = .135, corrected for degrees of freedom.

The ranking of the three economic variables remains the same; namely, the effect of the variable for the wife's earnings is larger than that for husband's predicted income, which in turn has an effect that exceeds (in absolute value) that of the transitory income component. The effect of the number of children (given the presence or absence of children under 6 years of age) is to decrease the probability of working full-time until this negative relation reaches a minimum at around 3 children. The mean number of children among this sample of wives who are in the labor force is 1.3 (standard deviation = 1.3). In other regressions (not shown) age, education, income history, urban residence, unemployment of the husband, and owning a house were all insignificant. The dummy variable for having remarried was, however, positive and significant. Its coefficient was 12.04 and its standard error, 5.84.

Disaggregated Regressions: Ratio of Years Worked While Married to Years Married as the Dependent Variable

The GAF survey data offer an opportunity to test the model of labor force participation on the work experience of wives over their entire married life. In chapter 2, I discussed the research of Morgan *et al.* in which "years worked while married" was regressed on six variables including the age and education of the wife (see Table 6). There is, as was noted, an obvious mechanical relation between the dependent variable and age of the wife, since older wives tend to have been married more years. To eliminate this relation, I use as a dependent variable the ratio of years worked while married to years married. The ratio takes on values from 0 to 1 inclusively. The results are shown in Table 29.

The principle finding of regressions I–III is that the education variable (or variables) is (are) positive and significant in contrast to the significant negative relation found in the study by Morgan *et al.* One reason for the difference (which actually is quantitatively unimportant here) is that the regressions in Table 29 include variables representing the economic status of the family (variables 2 or 3 and 11), which have the expected negative signs, and for which wife's education probably served in part as a proxy in the regression of the other study. A second and more important reason here is that their variable, "years worked while married," is positively related to years married, and since women with low education will be married more years (holding age constant), they will have worked more years while married.[65] Thus, education serves as a proxy for lateness of marriage, given the age of the wife. Clearly, using the ratio of years worked to years married avoids this confounding of effects and frees education to act in its proper role as a proxy for the wage effect.

The remaining variables require little comment:

(*a*) The same variable for "earnings capacity of the wife" that was used before is employed here, and it is significantly positive. It overpowers the education variables when all are included (columns IV–V), reducing the latter to insignificance. The variable for earnings capacity is especially rough in this context, of course, since it is often the wife's current occupation that is used to measure her past earnings ability. The coefficient of the variable is, in IV, .0146 and tells us that for each $100 increase in the wife's earnings abilities the ratio of years worked to years married increases by 1.5 percentage points. An effect of this magnitude is compatible with the effect of the same variable on the probability of the wife being in the labor force, which was shown in Table 26. The elasticity measure of the

[65] The interrelations among age of wife, age at marriage, education, and labor force experience are examined in Appendix F.

wife's earnings capacity on the ratio of her years worked while married is between 0.67 and 0.73, also in line with previous findings.

(*b*) Husband's predicted income and, more weakly, current family income (not including the wife's earnings) are considered proxies for the long-run income position of the family. (A socioeconomic score was tried here as a measure of the long-run economic position of the family and it proved to be utterly insignificant.) Surprisingly, the current family income figure has the stronger (negative) income effect. In terms of the dollar increase in income and associated decrease in percentage points of the ratio, however, all the coefficients on the income variables are small. For each $100 increase in family income (not including the wife's earnings) the ratio of years worked to years married declines by only .001 (or .1 percentage point). The fact that the regression coefficients and elasticities of the income measures are rather small probably is because they are poor measures of the long-run (lifetime) concept of income that the model calls for. On the other hand, the income effect may actually be smaller over the span of a long time period than we find it to be in predicting current labor force decisions. A small negative effect of income seems to prevail in the time series behavior of work by wives.

(*c*) Months pregnant, a proxy for the number of children ever born, has the largest t-value, and in conjunction with age accounts for 80 per cent of the R^2. Dividing the coefficient of months pregnant by 9 (in regression I for example), we see that the ratio of years worked decreases by about 0.11 for each "child." Since the mean of the ratio is about 0.34 the effect of the presence of additional children is considerable.

(*d*) The dummy variables for age detect the generally higher ratios among young wives. A ratio of 1 is much more likely, for example, among wives married one year than among the older wives married, say, 20 years.

(*e*) The highly significant positive coefficient on the variable for remarriage is evidence for the proposition that marital instability leads the wife to maintain closer ties to the labor force. (I should repeat that tastes factors may be causal to both marital instability *and* labor force participation, but that my original hypothesis concerned racial differences in work rates.) It is likely that this effect would appear stronger in the longer run context of Table 29 than in Table 26. "Months separated" has a positive sign but is not significant. "Separation" here included cases where the husband was in military service, however, and does not really reflect marital instability.

Some comments that summarize the over-all picture presented by the GAF data will be made at the end of this chapter. Prior to this, in the next section, research with the 1-in-1,000 sample is discussed.

TABLE 29

RESULTS OF REGRESSION ON YEARS WORKED/YEARS MARRIED BY THE WIFE: DISAGGREGATED DATA FROM GAF SURVEY[a]

Independent Variable	Units and Mean in Parentheses	Regression (Coefficients × 100) (Each Column Shows a Multiple Regression)				
		I.[b]	II.	III.	IV.	V.
1. Wife's earnings capacity	$00 (16.62)	....	....	....	1.33 (0.19) 0.67[c]	1.46 (0.20) 0.73[c]
2. Predicted husband's income	$00 (45.52)	− 0.10 (0.07) − 0.14[c]	....	....	− 0.14 (0.08) − 0.19[c]	− 0.05 (0.09) − 0.07[c]
3. Family income (not including wife's earnings)	$00 (47.03)	....	− 0.12 (.04) − 0.17[c]	− .10 (.04) − .14[c]	....	....
4. Months pregnant	months (19.20)	103. (6.)	100. (6.)	99. (6.)	95. (6.)	94. (6.)
5. Age variables[b]	....	d	d	d	d	d
6. Wife's education	years (11.32)	0.76 (.31)	e	e	f	f
7. Wife's education, squared	years (133.6)	....	e	e	f	f
8. Urban residence (during most of marriage)	1 if yes (0.76)	3.43 (1.56)	....	2.23 (1.90)	....	0.61 (1.90)
9. Ever remarried	1 if yes (0.09)	11.68 (2.25)	....	12.70 (2.79)	....	13.00 (2.76)
10. Months separated	months (3.32)	....	....	0.05 (0.09)	....	0.09 (0.09)
11. Income history, rising	1 if yes (0.50)	− 3.94 (1.33)	....	− 2.02 (5.08)	....	− 3.31 (5.02)
12. Income history, up and down	1 if yes (0.48)	....	....	2.21 (5.07)	....	2.28 (5.01)
R^2, corrected for degrees of freedom	....	.150	.142	.152	.158	.169

[a] Dependent variable: ratio of years worked while married to years married of 2,240 wives, white, aged 18–39, non-farm residents. Mean of the dependent variable is .337.

[b] For regression I, 21 dummies for age were used, one for each year, 18–38 (age 39 omitted). For regressions II–V, 10 dummies were used, one for each pair of years (ages 38–39 omitted).

[c] Elasticities at the mean.

[d] The F-ratio was significant at the 1 per cent level, where the test applied to the whole group of dummy variables for age.

[e] Education linear and education squared are so collinear that the standard error of each exceeds the coefficient. The relation of the two education terms with the ratio, years worked/years married of the wife, is positive, as follows:

$$\underset{(1.67)}{.16\,e} - \underset{(.08)}{.04\,e^2}$$

Nonetheless, together their F-ratio is highly significant. In the regressions II and III (II was an intermediate regression), the F-ratio was 5.01.

[f] The F-ratio for education and eduction squared in these regressions (which included "wife's earnings capacity") was .30, which is completely insignificant.

THE 1-IN-1,000 SAMPLE OF THE 1960 CENSUS

The interview data from this .1 per cent sample of the United States population taken from the 1960 census have two special attributes: the large number of observations (179,563) and the coverage of all races. From this sample, I selected white and Negro wives who had the following characteristics:

Husband present, and a civilian in the non-farm labor force
Between 14 and 65 years of age (inclusive) whose residence was either own house or a cash rental, excluding those who lived on a farm or in group quarters

After these exclusions the sample size was 26,831 – 24,788 white wives and 2,043 Negro wives.

Overview

Table 30 gives selected summary statistics for the observations, grouped by race, tenure, and husband's educational attainment. The two highest education groups among Negroes were combined to increase the numbers of observations. The first four columns give different measures of participation in the labor force. The racial differential is less pronounced using the "weeks-worked rate" rather than the current status, as shown in Table 31. This is one more piece of evidence that current rates of labor force participation overstate the labor supply of Negroes, and that a measure of weeks worked per year (or preferably hours worked per year) diminishes the extent by which Negro wives work more than white wives (see Appendix D for more evidence on this point).

The ratio of the wife's earnings capacity to family income (not including the wife's earnings) is shown in column 7 of Table 30. The term "earnings capacity" is used here because a wage-rate variable (average weekly earnings) has been multiplied by 50 to indicate full-time annual earnings (if the wife works the year around). The relation of this ratio to the weeks-worked, labor force participation rates (column 4) provides a quick, although rough, check on the income and wage effects and an interesting racial comparison. We expect that the participation rate should be directly related to the earnings ratio.

(*a*) White home-owners show a steeply falling ratio in column 7 (54 to 33 over-all) and in column 4 a fairly flat level of work rates except for a sharp dip for the highest education group (24 to 18 over-all). It takes relatively large increases in family income to reduce the wives' work rates and/or relatively minor increases in the wives' earnings to increase the rates.

TABLE 30

SELECTED SUMMARY STATISTICS FROM THE 1-IN-1,000 SAMPLE

Group: Race, Tenure, Education of Husband (Years)	Wives' Work Status				Family Income Minus Wife's Earnings	Working Wives' Average Weekly Earnings	Ratio of Wives' Earnings to Col. 5	Husband Unemployment Rate	Per Cent of Families With Children under 6 Years	Per Cent of Wives Who Have Remarried	Wife's Average Education	Number of Observations
	Average Weeks Worked	Current LFPR	1959 Employment Rate	1959 Weeks Worked Rate								
	(1)	(2)	(3)[a]	(4)[b]	(5)	(6)	(7)[c]	(8)	(9)	(10)	(11)	(12)
White Home-owners												
0- 4 years education	12.35	27	34	24	$ 5,242	$56.52	54	.070	14	18	6.6	401
5- 8	14.81	34	40	28	6,030	59.92	50	.045	11	13	9.3	3,944
9–11	15.59	35	43	30	6,649	66.54	50	.028	22	14	10.6	3,575
12	14.86	33	41	29	7,317	65.69	45	.017	42	11	11.6	4,702
13–15	14.55	32	39	28	8,663	69.80	40	.014	39	11	12.5	1,914
16 plus	9.49	23	29	18	11,410	75.07	33	.006	48	7	13.8	2,235
White Renters												
0- 4	9.84	26	30	19	4,137	55.73	67	.115	36	16	6.5	312
5- 8	15.30	36	44	29	4,765	57.50	60	.065	35	16	8.9	2,141
9–11	15.10	34	45	29	5,109	60.44	59	.060	46	13	10.3	1,873
12	17.03	36	49	33	5,266	62.58	59	.036	49	13	11.3	1,978
13–15	19.41	39	53	37	6,013	70.56	59	.026	46	12	12.3	821
16 plus	16.49	35	48	32	7,064	76.80	54	.007	50	8	13.8	892
Negro Home-owners												
0- 4	17.30	46	51	33	3,538	39.97	56	.087	19	23	6.4	149
5- 8	18.92	47	53	36	4,092	44.48	54	.073	25	26	8.4	315
9–11	17.88	46	52	34	4,465	53.89	60	.072	41	17	10.5	181
12	21.57	50	56	41	4,727	55.03	58	.044	38	16	11.0	136
13 plus	25.18	58	68	48	5,397	78.56	73	.011	46	13	13.2	94
Negro Renters												
0- 4	15.92	41	49	31	2,848	40.86	72	.053	41	24	7.0	206
5- 8	17.64	44	51	34	3,432	43.38	63	.078	43	21	8.4	438
9–11	16.16	40	47	31	3,663	48.60	66	.086	53	15	10.0	269
12	17.43	45	52	34	3,993	66.39	83	.056	50	10	10.8	196
13 plus	17.94	40	49	34	4,085	82.59	101	.068	54	15	12.1	59

[a] Column (3): per cent of wives having worked in 1959.

[b] Column (4): column 1 divided by 52.

[c] Column (6) was first multiplied by 50 before the division by column (5).

(*b*) Among Negro home-owners, the earnings ratio rises (56 to 73 over-all) and so do the participation rates (33 to 48 over-all). Although work rates of these Negro wives rise in the face of increasing family incomes, this rise is actually moderate given the very sharp increases in their earnings capacities.

(c) For white renters, the earnings ratio declines moderately from the low education group to the high (67 to 54) but is fairly constant over the middle four groups. The participation rate of the group with 0–4 years of education is unexpectedly low, then the rise is moderate over the middle four groups and dips (along with the earnings ratio) in the last one. With

TABLE 31

COMPARISON BY RACE OF TWO TYPES OF WORK RATES OF WIVES, BY TENURE AND EDUCATION OF THE HUSBAND (WHITE RATES AS PERCENTAGE OF NEGRO RATES)

Years of Education	Renters		Owners	
	Current Rates	Weeks Rates	Current Rates	Weeks Rates
0– 4	63	61	59	73
5– 8	82	85	72	78
9–11	85	94	76	88
12	80	97	66	71
13 plus	93	100	47	48

Source: Table 30.

this group rather slight increases in the wives' earnings along with moderate increases in the family income generate a consistent rise in work rates.

(*d*) Neither the earnings ratio (U-shaped) nor the participation rate (flat) moves systematically among Negro renters.

In general the rise in the wife's earnings capacity tends to exert a positive effect that overpowers the negative effect of the comparable rise in family income. The exceptions are the lowest education group and Negro renters.

Another noteworthy point observable in column 7 is the rise in earnings capacity of Negro wives' relative to Negro family incomes as education goes up, compared with white families. Furthermore, for each education-tenure group and ratio of Negro earnings to white earnings is quite different by sex, as is shown in Table 32. The first two columns of income ratios in Table 32 show the approximate relative effect of education on the earnings of Negro and white husbands since almost all of family income, excluding the wife's earnings, is income of the husband. The Negro males barely hold to their average ratio through 12 years of schooling. Their relative position worsens among the college-trained. Very nearly the reverse is true for wives. The earnings of Negro wives relative to white wives steadily improves as the educational levels of both rise, widening the gap between the female ratio shown and the family ratio.

The contrast between these trends and levels in ratios for the two sexes is startling. These ratios suggest another explanation for the higher work rates of Negro wives. The Negro wife earns a relatively high wage compared to the white wife who is her counterpart with respect to educational and tenure status—relatively high, that is, when contrasted with the

TABLE 32

NEGRO/WHITE INCOME AND EARNINGS RATIOS, BY TENURE AND EDUCATION OF THE HUSBAND

Years of Education	Family Income, N/W (Minus Wife's Earnings)		Working Wives Average Weekly Earnings, N/W	
	Owners	Renters	Owners	Renters
0– 4	67	69	71	73
5– 8	68	72	74	75
9–11	67	72	81	80
12	55	76	84	106
13 plus	53	62	108	112

Source: Table 30.

Negro-white comparison of the incomes of husbands. The regressions with SMA data did, of course, take into account both wives' and husbands' earnings, but perhaps they did not capture the pronounced unfavorable earnings position of the Negro husband compared with the wife that the stratification by education and tenure status brings out in Table 32.

The next question is why are these ratios as they are? Part of the answer may be that Negro wives tend to make more of a lifetime commitment to labor force attachment than white wives. As previously discussed, the differential effects of children and the conditions of housing and marital instability lead to this sustained attachment. A second reason for the more favorable picture for Negro females may well be that they face relatively less discrimination than Negro males, especially in the higher occupational levels. Both explanations appear reasonable to me, but the evidence at hand is insufficient for firm conclusions.

The rest of Table 30 goes over more familiar ground. We see the higher unemployment rates among Negro husbands, the higher incidence of remarriage among Negro wives, and their higher fertility rates (indicated by column 9). These comparisons are shown, of course, with the observed control over education and income status.

Main Regressions for White and Negro Wives, by Tenure Status

Now let us turn to the main group of regressions with the one-in-1,000 sample shown in Table 33. For each of the four race-tenure groups, two regressions were computed. In one the weeks worked by the wife during the year preceding (1959) is the dependent variable. In the other regression the dependent variable is the current labor force status of the wife. As discussed previously, the second regression is a linear probability model that predicts the probability that the wife will be in or out of the labor force.

The results of the regressions with data on white wives is straightforward. First, the two measures of labor supply as dependent variables are explained by the regressions in a very similar manner. Less variation in the current labor force status is accounted for (the R^2 is lower), and this is probably because it is a dichotomous variable. Weeks worked is a more nearly continuous variable, ranging between 0 and 52. (Means and standard deviations of the variables used in the regressions are listed in Table 38 in Appendix A.)

The variables for income of the family (excluding the wife's earnings), education of the wife, and the presence of children are all highly significant with the expected signs. By multiplying the arithmetic regression coefficient of income by the ratio of the means of the dependent and independent variables, the income elasticity was computed and is shown in Table 33. These are remarkably similar to the income elasticities of the 1960 SMA aggregates, shown in Table 15.

We also see that the income elasticity for white home-owners is larger (in absolute value) than that for white renters. The reason for this is not clear to me. It may be that families owning their own home are characteristically more wealthy and have higher debt obligations (particularly home mortgage payments). If this is true then the relatively high degree of responsiveness to income of work by the wife in this type of family may be explained as follows: when the husband's income is relatively high and the debts are well covered, the general affluence of the family permits the wife not to work. If, on the other hand, the husband's income is low for the given year, the contractual debt obligations compel the wife to work. This is in the spirit of the way Mincer has applied the ideas of permanent and transitory components of family income to the labor force behavior of wives.

TABLE 33

REGRESSION RESULTS WITH DISAGGREGATED DATA FROM THE 1-IN-1,000 SAMPLE OF WHITE AND NEGRO WIVES

Dependent Variable	R^2 (Corrected for Degrees of Freedom)	Independent Variable[a]										
		Constant	Family Income (Wife's Earnings $00)	Education[b] F-Ratio	Children[b] F-Ratio	Age[b] F-Ratio	Region	Size of Place		Husband Employed but Not at Work	Husband Unemployed	Wife Remarried
								Rural	Large Metropolitan Urban Area			
White home-owners												
Current status, 1960..	.132	19.7 (1.6)	− .19 (.07) − .45[c]	35	419	38	1.0 (.8)	.4 (.9)	.1 (.8)	3.5 (2.6)	5.0 (1.1)	5.2 (2.2)
Weeks worked, 1959..	.142	7.1 (.7)	−8.4 (.3) − .45[c]	33	509	42	.34 (.34)	− .3 (.4)	.46 (.34)	....	....	2.5 (.5)
White renters												
Current status, 1960..	.159	18.3 (2.6)	− .19 (.02) − .29[c]	11	334	19	− .14 (1.2)	−5.8 (1.5)	2.1 (1 .1)	6.2 (3.3)	5.4 (2.3)	6.6 (1.5)
Weeks worked, 1959..	.188	6.2 (1.1)	−9.0 (.7) − .30[c]	16	404	23	−1.0 (.5)	−2.8 (.6)	1.1 (.5)	....	....	2.1 (.6)
Negro home-owners												
Current status, 1960..	.091	34.8 (8.7)	− .14 (.07) − .13[c]	2.2	10	4	7.6 (3.8)	−8.9 (5.0)	5.7 (4.0)	3.4 (1.3)	8.3 (6.7)	10.0 (4.2)
Weeks worked, 1959..	.080	12.8 (3.8)	−2.6 (2.9)[d] − .06[c]	1.8	10	3	3.9 (1.7)	−4.0 (2.)	5.1 (2.)	....	....	5.1 (1.8)
Negro renters												
Current status, 1960..	.090	42.8 (7.8)	− .16 (.07) − .13[c]	2.8	18	1.4	7.1 (3.2)	−9.4 (6.1)	−12.7 (3.9)	−18.7 (12.4)	5.7 (5.5)	9.8 (3.8)
Weeks worked, 1959..	.100	12.2 (3.3)	−3.4 (2.8)[d] − .07[c]	1.7	25	1.4	3.7 (1.4)	−1.8 (2.6)	− 2.8 (1.6)	....	....	3.2 (1.6)

[a] Coefficients of the independent variables in regressions with current labor force status as the dependent variable are multiplied by 100. It is as if the "probability that the wife is in the labor force" is expressed as a labor force participation rate.

[b] Where sets of dummy variables are used, F-ratios are reported in place of regression coefficients. With the number of degrees of freedom in these samples, an F-ratio of 1.5 or over is signfiicant at the 5 per cent level and of 1.7 at the 1 per cent level. See Table 34 for the values of coefficients within the sets of dummies for "Education of Wife," "Children," and "Age of Wife."

[c] Elasticities at the mean.

[d] Note that the income coefficients in the regressions with weeks worked by Negro wives are insignificantly different from zero, so the income elasticities are not very meaningful.

A factor that runs in the opposite direction, however, is that renters are younger families with more young children, and we have come to expect a larger (negative) income effect for these families. (The age structure and per cent of families with and without young children is revealed in Table 38 where the means of the variables are listed.)

To determine the influence of education, children, and age, it is necessary to look at Table 34, which shows the coefficients of the dummy variables. The part of Table 34 dealing with the effects of education can illustrate how the table is to be read. The omitted variable is 12 years of school completed. For all other wives, then, we see the amount by which their labor force participation rates are above or below the rates of the wives who are high school graduates and who have gone no further in school. For example, for white wives who live in their own homes ("owners-current"), the labor force participation rates for those with 0–1 years of schooling completed are expected to be 24 percentage points lower than the rates of the high school graduates, holding constant all other variables in the model. Rates for wives who are college graduates (16 years or more of education) are, on net, higher by 12 percentage points, and so on.

Returning to Table 33 and the regression results for white wives, we see that unemployment of the husband has a significant positive effect. (Current unemployment of the husband was not considered an appropriate independent variable when weeks worked last year was the dependent variable.) Since unemployment of the husband is positively correlated with the area unemployment rate in the labor market relevant to the given family, the positive sign of husband's unemployment indicates that this stimulus to work by the wife is sufficiently strong to overcome the negative effect of the *area* unemployment. Recall that the census aggregative regressions show negative effects of area unemployment rates on area work rates of wives. But this was the net effect of unemployment across all families. With disaggregated data the specific effect on those families where the husband is unemployed is positive. There is no inconsistency between a negative effect of unemployment rates in aggregative regressions and a positive effect of unemployment of the husband in disaggregated regressions.

The variable for the husband being "with a job but not at work" bears only a slight similarity to unemployment.[66] The effect is positive, significant for renters and insignificant for owners.

[66] "With a job but not at work" includes those who did not work and were not looking for work, but had a job or business from which they were temporarily absent because of vacation, illness, industrial dispute, or bad weather, or because they were taking time off for various reasons. A large fraction of the husbands in this category are receiving full pay, so the income decline is much less than for the unemployed. Furthermore, the wife would not be expected to work when the husband has a vacation or is ill.

TABLE 34

Coefficients of Dummy Variables for Education and Age of the Wife and Absence of Children: Values from the Regressions Shown in Table 33

	White				Negro			
	Owners		Renters		Owners		Renters	
	Current[b]	Weeks	Current[b]	Weeks	Current[b]	Weeks	Current[b]	Weeks
Effects of "Education of the Wife"								
Education in years								
0– 1	—24.15	—9.52	—15.77	—10.59	—5.12[a]	—9.70	—48.50	—12.42
2– 4	—22.35	—10.01	—12.87	—7.02	—.13[a]	—5.82	—10.55[a]	—3.82
5– 7	—10.78	—5.54	—13.55	—7.49	2.27[a]	—2.79	—4.27[a]	—3.51
8	—8.36	—4.37	—5.31	—4.65	—10.14[a]	—4.03	—7.80[a]	—3.62
9–10	—4.05	—2.18	—6.74	—4.58	—1.42[a]	—6.37	—8.43	—2.01[a]
11	—3.38	—1.86	—6.36	—3.78	1.49[a]	—2.25[a]	.93[a]	.91[a]
12 (omitted)	....	....	....	....	....	....	....	....
13–15	5.64	1.95	1.41[a]	.98[a]	—6.76[a]	—2.33[a]	4.93[a]	2.69[a]
16 plus	12.13	3.88	9.73	3.44	28.45	7.65	38.09	14.58
F-ratios for set of dummy variables	38.41	42.14	18.75	23.35	3.83	3.18	1.37	1.38
Effects of "No Children Present by Specified Ages"[c]								
No children under 3	12.28	5.1	13.00	5.8	14.80	7.4	10.97	7.6
No children under 6	21.37	10.2	26.20	12.1	11.94	3.6	14.16	5.1
No children between 7–11	11.13	6.5	9.73	6.2	3.50[b]	1.9[a]	4.81[a]	2.1[a]
F-ratios for set of dummy variables	419.28	508.63	333.93	404.27	10.49	9.54	17.89	25.4
Effects of "Age of Wife"								
Age								
14–19	—9.25	—3.63[a]	—4.40[a]	—.28[a]	—16.09[a]	—6.13[a]	—5.26[a]	—7.49
20–24	1.12[a]	1.95	2.58[a]	5.20	4.40[a]	3.32[a]	—4.37[a]	—3.79[a]
25–29	1.07[a]	1.51	4.48	3.97	—7.77[a]	1.13[a]	—3.72[a]	—.28[a]
30–34	1.42[a]	2.13	4.72	3.63	—3.97[a]	2.92[a]	2.20[a]	—.94[a]
35–39	1.79[a]	1.07	2.52[a]	2.59	—5.35[a]	—2.33[a]	2.47[a]	—.84[a]
40–44 (omitted)	....	....	....	....	....	....	....	....
45–49	—3.39	—1.00[a]	—3.41[a]	—.43[a]	—14.67	—4.18[a]	—13.29	—5.48
50–54	—10.74	—4.63	—13.11	—3.38	—21.22	—5.87	—12.19[a]	—3.44[a]
55–59	—17.23	—7.03	—14.98	—5.21	—28.70	—10.62	—11.90	—5.04[a]
60–64	—27.14	—12.00	—27.80	—11.03	—45.30	—16.00	—12.82[a]	—6.01[a]
F-ratios for set of dummy variables	38.41	42.14	18.75	23.35	3.83	3.18	1.37[a]	1.38[a]

[a] Coefficients are *not* statistically significant. *t*-values are less than 1.96.

[b] Coefficients of the independent variables in the regressions with current labor force status as the dependent variable are multiplied by 100. It is as if the "probability of being in the labor force for each wife" were expressed as labor force participation rates.

[c] "No Children" was more convenient to use than combining the several categories of number of children into one variable for "Some Children."

The variable for remarriage is positive and significant. This is more support for the hypothesis that marital instability leads the wife to maintain closer ties to the labor force. But without better control over various tastes factors, we should exercise caution in interpreting this result.

The influence of the type and size of the place of residence is mixed, significant for renters but not among owners. The coefficients of the dummy variables for a rural place are negative, as expected, and for a large urban place (over 50,000 population), positive, as expected. The regional variable (1 if South, 0 otherwise) was insignificant.

No important differences between white renters and home-owners show up. Different effects of the independent variables are not indicated, and the generally low R^2's make it doubtful that variability stemming from the tastes factor (homework versus market work) was reduced. It appears that the separation by tenure adds very little to the analysis.

The regressions for Negro wives are not so easily interpreted as those for whites. They point to greater differences by race than did the aggregate census regressions. The income coefficient is significantly negative and similar to whites for regressions with current labor force status, but the variable lacks significance in regressions with weeks worked. Moreover, even for the regressions of current status, the elasticity measures are far lower than among whites—an opposite result from the SMA aggregate regressions.

A much larger number of the dummy variables for education and age are not significant with Negro wives. The very low R^2 of the regressions with Negro data, of course, is reflected by this. When the variables are significant they have the expected sign and ranking by size.

The lesser importance of the children variables in the case of Negro wives is consistent with previous findings. Table 34 indicates that it is the presence of relatively older children, between 7 and 11 years of age, however, that does not significantly deter Negro wives from work—a highly reasonable finding.

Southern residence has a positive effect, but the variable for size of place is mixed. Unemployment is positive but never significant, and "not at work" is both positive and negative in different regressions. The remarriage variable is significantly positive with larger coefficients than for whites.

Supplementary Regressions for White and Negro Wives, by Tenure Status and Education of the Husband

Separate regressions were run on each of the groupings by husband's education, within the race-tenure breakdown. These results, some of which are shown in Table 35, add a little more information about wage and income effects, but contribute little to explaining the differences by color.

One implication of Mincer's hypothesis on the effect of transitory income was not supported. The larger effect of the transitory component which Mincer found, implies that in those regressions where the transitory components are largest, the income effect will be largest (in absolute value). Conversely, the income effect will be smaller (in absolute value) when the permanent components are relatively larger. Holding the educational level of the husband constant reduces the variance of the permanent income component, so the transitory component is relatively larger. Table 35 shows the effects of income of the family and education of the wife in separate regressions for the different educational levels of the husband.

TABLE 35

PARTIAL REGRESSION COEFFICIENTS FOR INCOME (FAMILY INCOME MINUS WIFE'S EARNINGS) AND EDUCATION OF THE WIFE[a]

TENURE AND EDUCATION OF HUSBAND	WHITE		NEGRO	
	Income Coefficient	Education Coefficient	Income Coefficient	Education Coefficient
Home-owners				
0– 4.	− 7.4 (.3)	1.5 (.3)	−16.8 (7.5)	1.3 (.53)
	− .20 (.06)	.41 (.06)	− .60 (.18)	[c]
5– 8.	− 8.2 (.9)	1.1 (.1)	[c]	[c]
	− .17 (.02)	.22 (.03)	[c]	[c]
9–11.	− 9.7 (.9)	.8 (.2)	[c]	1.3 (.7)
	− .21 (.02)	.19 (.04)	[c]	.37 (.17)
12.	− 8.8 (.7)	1.3 (.2)	−24.6 (13.3)	[c]
	− .21 (.01)	.27 (.04)	[b]	[b]
13–15.	− 8.2 (.8)	.8 (.2)	[c]	[c]
	− .18 (.02)	.23 (.05)	[b]	[b]
16 plus. . . .	− 6.0 (.5)	.8 (.2)	[c]	[c]
	− .15 (.01)	.26 (.04)	[b]	[b]
Renters				
0– 4.	[c]	.6 (.3)	[c]	.96 (.43)
5– 8.	−10.1 (1.5)	.9 (.2)	[c]	[c]
9–11.	− 8.5 (1.6)	1.4 (.2)	[c]	[c]
12.	− 8.4 (1.6)	1.1 (.2)	[c]	[c]
13–15.	−10.1 (1.8)	1.4 (.4)	[c]	[c]
16 plus. . . .	− 7.7 (1.3)	1.3 (.3)	[c]	[c]

[a] Dependent variable in the top row of each group: weeks worked by the wife in 1959. This was the only regression for "Renters."

Dependent variable in the bottom row of each group: current labor force status of the wife in 1960. Coefficients of the independent variables have been multiplied by 100. It is as if "the probability that the wife is in the labor force" is expressed as a labor force participation rate.

[b] Because of technical difficulties with tapes and the computer no regressions were run with these groups.

[c] t-value less than 1.96.

The income effects are no larger than those reported in the regressions across all educational groups, where the variation of permanent components was greatest. Compare the coefficients of family income in Table 33 with those shown in Table 35.

The regression coefficients for the linear measure of education enable us to get some idea of the magnitude of the wage effect involved with these data. Ideally, we would like to know the wage rate equivalent of

TABLE 36

ANNUAL INCOME OF FEMALE INCOME RECIPIENTS, 25 YEARS OLD AND OVER, TOTAL AND AGED 45–54, BY EDUCATIONAL ATTAINMENT, 1963

YEARS OF SCHOOL COMPLETED			MEDIAN ANNUAL INCOME		AVERAGE INCREASE IN INCOME PER ADDITIONAL YEAR OF SCHOOLING	
(1) Bracket	(2) Mid-point[a]	(3) Increase Shown in Column 2	(4) All	(5) Aged 45–54	(6) All	(7) Aged 45–54
0– 7	5[a]	....	$ 851	$ 937	....	....
8	8	3	1,186	1,803	$112	$289
9–11	10	2	1,582	2,113	198	155
12	12	2	2,288	2,833	358	360
13–15	14	2	2,327	3,386	20	276
16	16	2	4,034	5,181	403	897
Median income			$1,611	$2,311		
Average increase in income per year of schooling (averaging the last two columns)					$218	$395
Average increase in income per year of schooling (dividing the difference between top and bottom figures by 11 years)					$289	$384

Source: Current Population Reports, "Consumer Income," Series P-60, No. 43, September 29, 1964.

[a] By far the largest number of women with 0–7 years of school completed have 6 and 7 years of schooling, so 5 is chosen as the mid-point rather than 3.5.

each year of education of the wife for the time of this survey. Annual earnings of full-time, year-round female workers, cross-tabulated by years of school completed, could serve as a proxy for a wage rate, but such information is not available, to my knowledge. In place of these measures we can use the income data of 1963 reported in Table 36.[67]

With these data we are able to estimate the annual dollar income per year of schooling. For the total group of females, 25 years of age and older,

[67] Income figures for 1963 were used because they included a cross-tabulation by age, which permitted a closer approximation to an earnings measure for females who worked full-time. This point is discussed in the next paragraph of the text.

who received income in 1963, the average increase in income per year of additional schooling was between $218 and $289 (see column 6 of Table 36). For females aged 45–54 the corresponding figures were $395 and $384. Females aged 45–54 had the highest incomes reported of any age group, and these figures appear to come closest to the measure of earnings for year-around, full-time female workers by education.[68]

The computation of wage elasticities is now straightforward. I will use the earnings figures for the group aged 45–54. These should be more reliable, and in any case they give lower, more conservative, estimates than the figures for total females. The measure of labor supply defined as "weeks worked in 1959" for white wives is used, since this is available for both renters and owners.

The typical coefficient for the education variable for "weeks worked" is 1.3, which implies that white wives worked an additional 1.3 weeks for each additional year of schooling they had completed. This is roughly equivalent to saying that for each $100 increase in annual wages wives worked a minimum of one-third (0.33) of a week more.[69] The elasticity at the mean of this measure is 0.51. This may be on the low side, not only because 0.33 is the smallest of the derived coefficients for "equivalent wages," but because the median income ($2,311) that multiplies the coefficient in the elasticity computation may be too low. The median earnings of female workers who worked full-time in 1963 was $3,592.[70] If this were used instead of $2,311, the wage elasticity would be 0.79 instead of 0.51.

All these estimates of a wage elasticity are very rough approximations, of course. They are intended mainly to provide checks on the general order of consistency with previous estimates. In this regard the results are reassuring. The estimated elasticity of wages is at least 0.51. This is smaller than the wage elasticity computed with the GAF data for 1955, (equal to 0.85), but then so were the 1960 elasticities lower than the 1950 measures for the aggregative data for SMA's.

Another interesting point to be made from the calculations based on

[68] As evidence, the median earnings of year-round, full-time female professional, technical, and kindred workers in 1963 was $5,100, and for private household workers, $1,240. These high and low medians correspond rather closely to the high and low income figures ($5,181 and $937) for the group aged 45–54 shown in column (5) in Table 36. (The source for the occupational earnings is Table 23 of *Current Population Reports*, Series P-60, No. 43, which is the source for Table 36 of the text.)

[69] The four measures of the earnings equivalent of a year of schooling are $395, $384, $289, and $218. These are "equal to" 1.3 weeks worked. Divide through by 3.95 (or 3.84, 2.89, or 2.18) and we get 0.33 (or 0.34, 0.45, or 0.60), respectively.

[70] Source: *Current Population Reports*, P-60, No. 43, Table 23.

Tables 35 and 36 is that the wage elasticity is slightly larger than the absolute value of the income elasticity, which ranged between −0.30 to −0.45 (from Table 33). This also agrees with the GAF survey data.

General Comments on the Regressions with Disaggregated Data

Two samples of survey data were used for statistical analysis in this chapter. The 1-in-1,000 sample of the 1960 census has an exceedingly large number of observations. The research I conducted with this sample is only a start in exploiting this rich source. The survey data from the Growth of American Families study constituted a "small" sample relative to the 1-in-1,000 sample, but it proved to be quite flexible for the purposes of this study. The availability of the "predicted income" of the husband as an income variable, of "potential earnings" of the wife as a wage variable, and the information on the labor force experience of the wife over her entire married life all added somewhat unique and, I think, important content to this study.

An effort was made to organize the survey data in a form to which the economic model could apply efficiently.[71] For example, the model postulates a substitution effect from variations in the wage rate that applies to the wife. To represent the wage rate a variable, labeled "potential earnings," was constructed with the GAF data in order to approximate the theoretical concept more closely than achieved with the variable, years of school completed. From the regressions with the 1-in-1,000 sample, the coefficients from the education variable were translated into a wage elasticity that agreed with the previous findings.

The GAF data also enabled the resolution of the puzzle posed by the negative relation between the education of the wife and the number of years she worked. First it was shown that education and years married (holding age constant) are negatively related. This explained why Morgan *et al.* got a negative sign for education when this was a variable in a regression predicting "years worked while married." Next, the ratio of years worked over years married was tried as a dependent variable, and a positive relation was found between this measure of the "lifetime" supply of labor and the wife's education.

The effects of different measures of family income were consistently

[71] The term, "efficiently," may seem inappropriate when discussing statistical applications of a model in which the multiple correlations were so low. But remember that survey data will reflect the enormous variation in a great many personal characteristics, like tastes, that are not captured by the variables at hand. And, unless it can be shown that the omissions bias the coefficients of the included variables, this may be of no great concern.

negative on the labor supply of the wife. Income elasticities were similar in size between the two samples. With the GAF data the income elasticity for family income (excluding the wife's earnings) was −0.47 (see Table 26), and the comparable elasticity for white wives in the 1-in-1,000 sample lay between −0.29 and −0.45 (see Table 33).

In general we can say that the effects of the economic variables behaved as expected in the analyses of disaggregated data. The experiment with grouped data from the GAF sample offered more confirmation (pp. 89–91). The sizes of the income elasticities and the approximations computed for wage elasticities point to substitution effects that are similar to those computed with aggregative data for SMA's. A direct application of formulas (4) and (5) for the "pure" substitution effect (see pp. 12–13) is blocked by, first, the lack of an elasticity of non-labor income and, second, the imprecise measures available from the survey data for the relation between the wife's earnings and the husband's earnings.[72]

With the GAF data the effect of the transitory component of income was negative but somewhat smaller than the effect of "permanent" or "predicted" income. The 1-in-1,000 sample showed no difference in the two effects in tests that involved separate regressions on groups where transitory (or, alternatively, permanent) income components varied in relative magnitude. One suggested reason for this finding is that when a transitory income decline does not solely reflect unemployment of the husband, the positive effect on the wife's decision to work may not be so large, since a homework substitute is not potentially available. Another reason for a small transitory effect, applying to both GAF and 1-in-1,000 samples, may be a large amount of errors of measurement in the reported income figures. To repeat, these error components would have, by definition, a zero slope. If included in the transitory component they would tend to pull down the "true" transitory income effect. Another source of difficulty in handling the hypothesis and in interpreting the results lies in distinguishing between expected and unexpected transitory changes in income. Life-cycle transitory components (negative for workers in their early 20's, positive during the ages between 45 and 60, for example) are mostly expected, whereas unemployment and illnesses usually are not. The effect of these two types of transitory components may be different and, if so, it would be necessary to distinguish between them.

With these survey data most of the variation in labor force behavior could be explained on the basis of the presence and number of children and

[72] The low correlations between the wife's and husband's wage, characteristic of disaggregated data in cross-sections, do not permit reliable estimates for the changes in income shares as the wife's wage varies (see pp. 51–52).

the age of the wife. This was, by and large, ordinary fare. Some, but perhaps too little, experimentation was made with different functional forms and interaction effects involving these variables. In one case, using GAF data, important interactions between economic factors and the presence of children under 6 years of age was demonstrated (see Table 27).

The variable to denote whether the wife remarried was a less familiar sociodemographic characteristic, and it was found to have a positive effect on work by the wife during her married life (GAF data) and was highly significant in those regressions from the 1-in-1,000 sample that involved white wives. It had an even larger effect on the labor force participation of Negro wives. These results bolster the hypothesis that a tendency toward marital instability will induce more market work by the wife. For this reason Negro wives would have higher levels of labor force participation, since family instability is relatively prevalent among Negroes.

IV

Conclusions

Summary and Interpretations

This study of the labor force participation of married women builds upon an impressive foundation of prior research. The works of Jacob Mincer and Marvin Kosters in particular provided models that, with slight modifications, I applied to a wider range of data than heretofore examined. The sources of data for statistical analyses were ample.

The over-all problem is one of explaining labor force participation of married women. At the center is the challenge of explaining the increase in participation over time. We began with two basic propositions from price theory on the effects of income and of wages on the supply of labor. An economic model was set up to deal with two types of available data. The first type consisted of aggregative data, and the model incorporated market variables—average labor force participation rates, average income, average wages, and so on. These market variables correspond to the observations we have in mind when discussing the time series increase. An advantage of the data in this form is that the wide variations in preferences or tastes for and against market work among women can be greatly reduced in the process of averaging. The principal disadvantage is the "identification problem"—the danger that responses in labor force participation rates to changes in wage rates engender feed-back effects that modify the wage and thereby cloud the interpretation of the statistical results.

The second application of the model was with disaggregated data. Here we are given almost no information on market variables but instead work with the personal characteristics of the subject. The troublesome problem lies in distinguishing between the effects of variables that impinge upon the wife's decisions from those that merely reflect her decisions—perhaps via some factor like tastes that is common to both the decision and to the variable in question. The low multiple correlations common to regressions with survey data may not be cause for alarm, but they do tell us that there are missing variables that could greatly add to the explanatory power of the relation. We hope, but we cannot feel sure, that these omitted variables are uncorrelated with the included variables.

The economic model was, thus, made to do double duty, handling market data in one case and individual or personal data in another. Although specific criteria for judgment are lacking, I believe the agreement of the results between the two applications was considerable. Indeed, there was about as much agreement between the results from the regression analysis with aggregated and disaggregated data as there was among different samples within each of the two types of data. Confining our attention to results with total or white wives, recall that the elasticities (or logarithmic coefficients) of variables representing the wife's wage with aggregated data varied from about 1.0 (with SMA's in 1950) to around .4 or .5 (with aggregated data from the 1955 GAF sample, cities in 1940, and SMA's in 1960). From the disaggregated data the approximations of the wage elasticity varied from around .8 (the GAF sample) to .5 (the 1-in-1,000 sample).

Income elasticities based on the logarithmic coefficients of either the husband's earnings or family income (excluding the wife's earnings) were remarkably stable from sample to sample. The coefficients of husband's income were about −.4 to −.6 for each of the samples of aggregative data—1940 cities, 1950 and 1960 SMA's, and the "cluster points" with the 1955 GAF survey data. The elasticities computed with disaggregated data ranged between −.3 and −.7.

One of the principal issues in the explanation of the increase in work rates by wives over time involves the comparative sizes of the elasticities of wages and income. Since the earnings of females and males have been rising by about the same rate over time, an explanation for the secular increase in work rates is that the positive effect on the labor supply of the rise in wages outweighs the negative effects of the rise in incomes. The major finding made by Mincer was that, for wives, the positive wage effect exceeds the absolute value of the negative income effect. This finding was weakened by my research but not overturned. The result held for 1950 with the aggregative data that were essentially the same as Mincer used, but in 1940 and 1960 the income elasticity was sometimes larger than the wage elasticity. With disaggregated data the wage elasticity was larger than the income elasticity in each of the two samples used, but the estimation procedures for the wage effect were, by necessity, quite rough.

Lower wage elasticities relative to income elasticities indicate that less of the time series increase in work rates of married women can be explained by these two variables.[1] Nevertheless, the positive direction of

[1] See Mincer's application of cross-section coefficients of income and wages to time series data from 1900–1950. Jacob Mincer, "Labor Force Participation of Married Women," in *Aspects of Labor Economics, A Conference of the Universities*, National Bureau of Economic Research (Princeton: Princeton University Press, 1962), p. 93.

change in the time series agrees with that generally predicted by the cross-section results for wage and income effects (see Table 24). The findings about female educational attainment add supporting evidence of two sorts. First, a positive effect of education on the labor force participation of wives was established with cross-section data, and the increase of both education and participation over time is consistent with this finding. Second, the hypothesis of a large wage effect for wives is supported since education is a variable that partly captures the non-pecuniary returns to labor—fringe benefits, pleasant working conditions, and so forth.

Two additional results from the analyses of the census aggregations may be mentioned. (*a*) The effect of unemployment on the labor force participation of wives was consistently negative (although not significantly so in regressions with nonwhite wives). Several checks were made that reinforced this finding. In combination with similar results for other secondary workers (see Appendix J), this leads to a rejection of the "added worker hypothesis." A positive relation between low unemployment rates and wives' work rates contributes to an explanation of the rise in work rates from the depression decade, 1930–40, to the period of tighter labor markets from 1942 on, but it is difficult to determine the quantitative impact here, since the cross-section effect of unemployment does not transfer to a long-run time series very readily. (*b*) The presence of children had a consistently negative effect. This is consistent with the trend of lower birth rates and more market work by wives up to 1940. On the other hand, the problem of reconciling the time series and cross-sectional relations from 1940 to 1960 is made more difficult.

It is tempting to suggest that in cross-sections the presence of young children and abstention from market work by the mother reflect decisions only about the timing of work, and that these abstentions may occur even though both fertility rates and work during some part of the married life may be increasing over time. This explanation is not sufficient, however. Recall that the work rates of mothers of young children have been increasing over time (see Table 2), which indicates that either the presence of children is less inhibiting to work than before or that other factors more than offset the negative effect of the presence of children.

The time series increase in work by married women remains only partially explained. A more complete explanation requires more information about the interrelations of work, wage rates, and fertility, about changes in work in the home, about the non-pecuniary aspects of market work, and about changes in attitudes (or tastes).

A general comment about the use of disaggregated data is that the theoretical expectations of the basic economic model were corroborated with a variety of measures of the labor supply of wives. Wage effects were positive, income effects were negative, and so on. With the GAF data several measures of supply—the current labor force status of the wife, the lifetime work experience of wives, and the extent of participation—all performed favorably. With the 1-in-1,000 sample, two measures—weeks worked and the current status—both gave similar results that were also in agreement with the predictions of the model.

The analysis made of the labor force behavior of nonwhite wives showed similar patterns to those for white (or "total") wives, although there were differences between the two color groups that called for special attention. Over time, work rates of white wives have increased more rapidly than those of nonwhite wives. On this point I noted the large proportion of the nonwhite female labor force in domestic service, the declining trends of this occupation, and the impact this would have on the time series of participation rates of nonwhite wives. In addition we can point to the findings from regression analyses of larger income effects relative to wage effects for nonwhite wives in comparison with white wives. These were consistent with the slower rate of increase in work rates of nonwhite wives over time. The explanation for the differences in wage and income effects is not, however, evident.

At a moment-in-time we consistently observe two related differences in the labor force behavior of nonwhite and white wives: higher levels of labor force participation over-all among nonwhite wives, and higher work rates for nonwhite mothers of young children. Four explanations of these differences were suggested, each along with some supporting empirical evidence.

(1) The simplest point is that labor force participation *rates* overstate the amount of labor supplied by nonwhite wives compared with white wives, since the latter are more likely to be working more hours per week or weeks per year if working at all. Nonwhite females are disproportionately represented in service occupations, particularly domestic service, that involve part-time work. Their occupational characteristics in turn reflect relatively low educational attainments, lesser training, and market discrimination.

(2) Poorer housing conditions, smaller dwelling units, and more doubling up of families among nonwhites are all generally conducive to more market work and less homework by wives.

(3) Relative instability of nonwhite families leads the wife to maintain closer ties to the labor market. This tendency is reinforced by her typically low income status and limited chances of obtaining alimony or adequate financial support for her children.

(4) Finally, the nonwhite husband may face greater discrimination in the labor market than the wife, leading to some substitution in market

work between them. It is unlikely that this disadvantage to the male would be entirely captured in the measures of his earnings and unemployment experience that were included in my analyses.

Two points are noteworthy about the foregoing list. One is that they are interrelated and reinforcing. The second is that all of them contribute to explaining both the higher levels of participation among nonwhite wives *and* the lesser importance of children as a deterrent to work. In fact, I should say that in explaining the second question you explain the first.

The uses of disaggregated data to analyze differences in labor force behavior between white and Negro wives had ambivalent results. Two findings aid in reconciling the differences. First, the white wives in the GAF sample and both white and Negro wives in the 1-in-1,000 sample who had remarried were more likely to be working than wives who married only once, holding many other variables constant. This result supports the hypothesis that the prevalance of marital instability among nonwhite wives is a reason for their high work rates. Second, the multiple regression with the 1-in-1,000 sample indicated that, with control over many important variables, the presence of children under 3 years of age was about as deterring to work among Negro wives as among white wives; that the presence of children under 6 years of age was only slightly less deterring to Negro wives; and only when children aged 7 to 11 were present did Negro wives work more readily than white wives. This finding carries us one step closer to an understanding of what at first appeared to be a major difference between white and Negro wives. Given the prevalence of part-time work among Negro wives, it is not surprising that children of school age would not be much of a barrier to work by the mother. And the observed higher work rates of the Negro mothers of preschool age children seem to be accounted for by the other economic and demographic variables in my analyses.

On the other hand, the regression results for the sub-sample of Negro wives from the 1-in-1,000 sample are in a somewhat unsettled state. The variation in work explained was uncomfortably small by comparison with the tests with the data for white wives from the same source. From the economist's point of view, the weak performance of income and wage (i.e., education) effects, which were correct in sign but sometimes lacking in statistical significance, was disconcerting.

Some Implications

I will conclude by pointing to a few implications of this study for some current theoretical and policy issues. Married women have become so important a segment of the labor force that attention to their work patterns is necessary for a full understanding of many important economic problems: economic growth and the cyclical behavior of national income, the personal distribution of income, the effects of income taxes on labor supply, and birth rates.

Consider first the effect of unemployment conditions on labor force participation. It was noted many times that the elasticity of the supply of labor will be relatively high for wives and, probably, for other secondary workers who similarly possess good alternatives to leisure and market work. Decreases in the wage rate are likely to result in relatively large decreases in the quantity of labor supplied. This prediction is consistent with the result in cross-sections of a reduction in labor supplied for areas of depressed business conditions or high unemployment. If these results apply to the time series, the rather high national rates of unemployment of recent years (1958–63) may, therefore, be an important cause of the decline in labor force participation of several groups of secondary workers.[2] This decline in participation, moreover, is surely part of the explanation of the slow-down in the rate of growth of the Gross National Product during these years. Now, a decline in GNP is not necessarily a decline of equal magnitude in the well-being of the population, particularly when unmeasured homework (or school work) may be increasing. Nevertheless, the withdrawal from the labor force of secondary workers in the face of high unemployment can be the source of economic hardship, particularly in depressed areas.[3]

Renewed interest in the question of the distribution of income in general and the problem of low incomes in particular calls for special attention to the role of secondary workers like wives. At the upper end of the income distribution, we see that 64 per cent of families in 1960 earning $10,000 or more had two or more earners.[4] At the other end of the income scale where unemployment is an important cause of low income, secondary workers often provide the means for economic solvency. Referring to a survey of families with the head of the household unemployed 5 weeks or more in 1961, Ewan Clague, former Commissioner of Labor Statistics, stated:

[2] See the discussion of this decline in the Report of the President's Committee to Appraise Employment and Unemployment Statistics, *Measuring Employment and Unemployment* (Washington, D.C.: Government Printing Office, 1963), pp. 69–72.

[3] See the findings of Martin Segal and Richard B. Freeman, *Population, Labor Force, and Unemployment in Chronically Depressed Areas* (U.S. Department of Commerce, Economic Analysis Division, Office of Planning and Research, Area Redevelopment Administration, 1964).

[4] U.S. Census of Population, 1960, Subject Reports, "Sources and Structure of Family Income," Table 1, p. 1.

> Additional workers in the family constitute the greatest single bulwark against poverty through unemployment. . . . Most of these families had some nonwage income, but the amounts were small in relation to the wage and salary incomes of family workers.[5]

Another important issue concerns the effect of the personal income tax on the household's work decisions. The economist's analysis of this problem calls for determining whether the substitution effect of the tax on work reduces the supply of labor more or less than the income effect of the tax increases the supply of labor. The impression obtained from prior research is that the income tax does not reduce the quantity of labor supplied, but the evidence pertains mainly to primary earners.[6] Wage or substitution effects are expected to be small among primary earners, but not for secondary workers, so the effects of taxation may be different for the latter. Indeed, on the basis of the evidence at hand, the substitution effect appears to outweigh the income effect of the tax, and a net deterrence to work is implied. One qualification, however, is that the suggested special importance of non-pecuniary aspects of employment for wives and, perhaps, other secondary workers provides a means of avoiding the incidence of the tax, since payment for work in this form is not taxed. These remarks are highly tentative, however. More information on the impact of various marginal rates of the progressive income tax is needed, and more precise estimates of income and substitution effects than those offered in this study are called for.

Finally, the relation between female wages, work rates, and birth rates needs to be explored much more fully to determine the partial effect of changes in wages on fertility. Advances in the means of birth control will permit greater personal choice in decisions about family size and, I would argue, more scope for the influence of economic variables. At the same time there is a growing concern over the size and density of the population. It is not necessary to dwell on the importance of these issues.

[5] Ewan Clague, "Anatomy of Unemployment," speech before the Conference of Business Economists, New York, May 8, 1964, unpublished. The survey referred to by Clague is described in U.S. Department of Labor, Bureau of Labor Statistics, "Special Labor Force Report No. 37," Reprint No. 2430. Table B on page A-8 of this report showed that among the families surveyed, the median earnings of family members other than the head of the household contributed 26 per cent ($1,564) of total family income; that non-wage sources (like unemployment compensation) added 16 per cent; and the rest was the earnings of the head during the period when he was not unemployed. The wife was most likely to be the supplementary earner in these families.

[6] See Marvin Kosters, "Income and Substitution Parameter in a Family Labor Supply Model" (Ph.D. dissertation, University of Chicago, 1966) for a brief review of the literature and for his estimates of wage effects on the labor supply of males aged 50–64, which support the conclusion that the substitution effect for males is small.

APPENDIX A

The Variables Used in Regressions with Census Data

GLOSSARY OF SYMBOLS FOR CENSUS AGGREGATES

m labor force participation rate of married women, husband present, during the census week (in per cent)

The next nine variables are measured in hundreds of dollars; and all income and earnings figures apply to the year preceding the census.

y median income for male family heads, spouse present

w median income of females who worked 50–52 weeks in the year preceding the census

y' median income of all males with income

w' median income of all females with income

y'' median earnings of the male civilian labor force

y_{52} median income of males who worked 50–52 weeks in the year preceding the census

y_n referred to as non-labor income; the median income other than wage and salary earnings and earnings from self-employment, per recipient over 14 years of age in 1950 and per person in 1960 (among all persons who received any income in 1959)

w'' median earnings of the female civilian labor force

w''' median full-year earnings of the female civilian labor force (Defined as: the median income of the female labor force, divided by the average weeks worked by females who worked, multiplied by 51. Used for nonwhites only)

c per cent of husband-wife families with one or more children under 18 years of age

c' per cent of husband-wife families with one or more children under 6 years of age (Note: for 1960, c' applies to all families)

c'' number of children under 5 years of age per 100 women ever married

c''' number of children ever born per 1,000 women ever married

u male unemployment rate (in per cent)

u_f female unemployment rate (in per cent)

u' per cent of the male labor force who worked less than 27 weeks in 1949

u'' per cent of the male labor force, aged 35–44, who worked less than 50 weeks in 1959

u_t male unemployment rate defined with the total population of males eligible to be in the labor force in the denominator (per cent)

r dummy variable for the region of the U.S.: "1" is a southern SMA or city; "0" otherwise

e median years of schooling completed by females, 25 years and older

e' per cent of the population aged 25 years and older with a completed high school education (Note: used only in tables reproduced from the study of Jacob Mincer)

ind the per cent of the civilian labor force engaged in mining, construction, agriculture and related industries, business and repair services, transportation, communication, and durable manufacturing industries (Note: constitutes a "male-demanding" industrial structure)

n the per cent nonwhite in the SMA

woh the per cent of husband-wife families without their own household

mg the per cent of the population who are in-migrants (i.e., lived in a different county five years ago)

ΔL percentage change in total non-agricultural employment in the SMA from the year preceding to the year of the census

Δp percentage change in population of the SMA from 1950 to 1960

a_{65} per cent of the population in the SMA 65 years of age or older

TABLE 37

SOURCES, MEANS, AND STANDARD DEVIATIONS OF VARIABLES USED IN REGRESSIONS WITH CENSUS AGGREGATIVE DATA

VARIABLE	YEAR*	TOTAL			NONWHITE		
		Mean†	Standard Deviation†	Source Followed by Table Number	Mean†	Standard Deviation†	Source Followed by Table Number
m	1960	31.25	3.80	[a]C-33	42.91	7.29	[a]D-105, D-116
	1950	22.90	4.04	[c]183	35.62	7.17	[d]70
y	1960	52.17	5.63	[a]D-135	....	....	....
	1950	31.05	2.95	[f]D-11	....	....	....
y'	1950	27.21	3.21	[c]185	18.63	3.47	[c]185
	1940	11.81	1.72	[f]D-10	....	....	....
y''	1960	49.12	5.44	[a]D-130	32.72	7.01	[a]D-130
y_{52}	1960	55.53	5.43	[a]D-136	....	....	....
	1950	27.21	3.19	[f]D-11	....	....	....
y_n	1960	4.23	.91	[k]	....	....	....
	1950	6.48	1.30	[d]93	....	....	....
w	1960	32.00	3.96	[a]D-136	....	....	....
	1950	20.14	2.47	[f]D-11	....	....	....
w'	1950	12.02	2.43	[c]185	8.60	2.31	[c]185
	1940	7.06	1.36	[f]D-10	....	....	....
w''	1960	23.46	3.69	[a]D-130	15.00	4.76	[a]D-130
w'''	1960	....	....	....	21.01	6.32	[a]D-130, D-118
c	1950	53.13	3.38	[e]36	43.48	4.62	[e]37
c'	1960	31.77	3.31	[a]C-32	35.98	4.54	[a]D-110
	1950	32.26	2.57	[e]40	....	....	....
c''	1940	21.44	2.22	[h]37	....	....	....
c'''	1960	2367.	201.	[a]D-113	2574.	267.	[a]D-113
u	1960	5.47	4.10	[a]D-115	9.42	3.21	[a]D-115
	1950	5.29	1.75	[c]89	9.17	3.28	[d]66
	1940	11.63	2.79	[g]66	....	....	....
u_t	1960	3.95	3.94	[p]143	....	....	....
u_f	1950	4.63	1.72	[c]89	....	....	....
	1960	5.24	1.45	[a]D-115	....	....	....
u'	1950	12.96	2.53	[c]72	....	....	....

* The 1960 data do not include Honolulu. The designation "nonwhite" in that metropolitan area would generally mean Asian rather than Negro populations.

† The means and standard deviations are listed in the units in which the variables were entered in the regressions, which are indicated in the Glossary on pp. 123–24.

[a] State volumes of the 1960 Census. Series identifications, C or D, is noted above along with the table number.

[b] Summary volume of national population statistics, Series A, of the 1960 Census.

[c] *1950 Census, General Characteristics of the Population*, Vol. II., Part 1: U.S. Summary.

[d] *1950 Census*, State volumes, *General Characteristics of the Population*, Vol. II, Parts 2–50.

[e] *1950 Census, General Characteristics of Families*, Special Report.

[f] Gertrude Bancroft, *The American Labor Force* (New York: John Wiley and Sons, 1958). (Tables D-5 and D-10 of this source are standardized for the age composition of the metropolitan area.)

[g] *1940 Census, Characteristics of the Population*, Vol. II, Part 1: U.S. Summary.

[h] W. H. Graybill, C. K. Kiser, and P. K. Whelpton, *The Fertility of American Women* (New York: John Wiley and Sons, 1958). (Table 37 of this source is standardized for the age composition of the cities.)

[j] See Table 42 in Appendix B of this book.

[k] Figures for non-labor income are based on Table 76 in Series D of the 1960 Census. They were obtained from William G. Bowen and T. Aldrich Finegan of Princeton University.

[m] Bureau of Labor Statistics, *Employment and Earnings*, 1939–63.

[n] *United States Census, 1960, United States Summary, Detailed Characteristics.*

[p] *United States Census, 1960, United States Summary, General Social and Economic Characteristics.*

TABLE 37—*Continued*

VARIABLE	YEAR*	TOTAL: Mean†	TOTAL: Standard Deviation†	TOTAL: Source Followed by Table Number	NONWHITE: Mean†	NONWHITE: Standard Deviation†	NONWHITE: Source Followed by Table Number
u''	1960	23.99	6.93	[n]300	....	....	....
r	1960	.29	.46	....	.42	.50	....
	1950	.26	.44	....	.52	.51	....
	1940	.27	.45	....	....	....	....
e	1960	11.15	.84	[a]C-73	9.21	1.04	[a]D-103
	1950	10.32	1.07	[d]65	8.08	.96	[d]65
	1940	9.26	1.08	[g]60	....	....	....
ind	1950	39.66	8.75	[j]	....	....	....
n	1960	10.00	9.00	[b, a]C-77	....	....	....
	1950	8.84	8.50	[e]86	....	....	....
woh	1960	2.12	.71	[a]C-32	4.50	1.20	[a]C-77
mg	1960	18.70	11.19	[a]C-32	13.70	8.60	[a]C-77
ΔL	1960	2.20	3.38	[m]	....	....	....
Δp	1960	34.04	36.40	[b]A-31	....	....	....
a_{65}	1960	8.61	1.88	[a]C-33	....	....	....

TABLE 38

MEANS AND STANDARD DEVIATIONS OF VARIABLES USED IN THE REGRESSIONS WITH THE 1-IN-1,000 SAMPLE FROM THE 1960 CENSUS (STANDARD DEVIATIONS ARE IN PARENTHESES)

VARIABLE	WHITE				NONWHITE			
	Home-owners		Renters		Home-owners		Renters	
1. Weeks worked by wife in 1959	14.19	(20.65)	16.02	(20.92)	19.51	(21.62)	16.97	(20.93)
2. Current labor force participation rate[a].....	32.26	(46.75)	35.41	(47.82)	48.67	(49.98)	42.72	(49.47)
3. Family income (excluding wife's earnings)	$7,521	(4,996)	$5,328	(3,355)	$4,314	(2,681)	$3,509	(2,203)
4. Education, years completed[b]								
0– 1......	.002	(.048)	.005	(.073)	.009	(.091)	.009	(.010)
2– 4......	.011	(.105)	.021	(.145)	.079	(.270)	.055	(.228)
5– 7......	.064	(.245)	.083	(.276)	.187	(.390)	.188	(.390)
8.........	.115	(.319)	.134	(.341)	.123	(.329)	.154	(.361)
9–10......	.159	(.365)	.190	(.393)	.202	(.402)	.224	(.417)
11.........	.063	(.243)	.073	(.259)	.080	(.271)	.106	(.308)
12[d].........	.399		.353		.189		.218	
13–15......	.119	(.324)	.089	(.285)	.071	(.257)	.033	(.180)
16+......	.068	(.252)	.052	(.223)	.059	(.236)	.013	(.113)
5. Families without children:[b]								
Under 3 yrs. of age......	.79	(.41)	.67	(.47)	.79	(.41)	.65	(.48)
Under 6 yrs. of age......	.65	(.48)	.56	(.49)	.68	(.47)	.53	(.50)
Between 7–11 yrs. of age.........	.62	(.49)	.73	(.44)	.65	(.48)	.70	(.46)
6. Husband unemployed[b]....	.026	(.158)	.048	(.214)	.064	(.245)	.071	(.257)
7. Husband not at work[b]........	.017	(.131)	.022	(.147)	.016	(.123)	.013	(.113)
8. Wife remarried	.12	(.32)	.13	(.34)	.21	(.41)	.18	(.39)
9. Region[b] (South).......	.26	(.43)	.24	(.43)	.59	(.49)	.46	(.50)
10. Residence[b]								
Rural nonfarm.......	.23	(.42)	.17	(.38)	.17	(.38)	.07	(.27)
Large city[c]..	.32	(.47)	.50	(.50)	.53	(.50)	.75	(.43)
Small city[d]..	.45		.33		.30		.18	
11. Age of wife[b]								
14–19......	.006	(.008)	.053	(.224)	.029	(.167)	.045	(.208)
20–24......	.051	(.220)	.202	(.401)	.047	(.211)	.170	(.375)
25–29......	.107	(.309)	.160	(.366)	.110	(.313)	.165	(.371)
30–34......	.157	(.364)	.129	(.335)	.138	(.345)	.182	(.386)
35–39......	.179	(.383)	.116	(.320)	.155	(.362)	.010	(.341)
40–44[d]......	.244		.097		.156		.234	
45–49......	.131	(.338)	.090	(.287)	.129	(.335)	.080	(.272)
50–54......	.010	(.299)	.074	(.262)	.122	(.328)	.064	(.245)
55–59......	.074	(.262)	.050	(.217)	.081	(.276)	.036	(.186)
60–64......	.041	(.199)	.029	(.168)	.033	(.179)	.014	(.116)

[a] Current labor force status is, for each wife, a probability that she will be in the labor force. The mean for this variable is the participation rate divided by 100.

[b] For dummy variables the mean is the proportion of wives in the sample with the given characteristic.

[c] A large city was a city of 50,000 population or more. A small city had 2,000 to 49,000 population.

[d] The omitted dummy variable.

APPENDIX B

Supplementary Tables

Tables 39–41 show several comparisons of labor force participation rates of white and nonwhite wives with the income of the husband as the principal control variable.

Table 42 shows the per cent of female employment in the major industries in the United States in 1949. This table became the basis for the definition of the variable, *ind*, measuring the industrial structure in the SMA.

TABLE 39

PROPORTION OF MARRIED WOMEN AGED 35–44 IN THE LABOR FORCE IN 1940, BY COLOR, RESIDENCE, AND INCOME OF THE HUSBAND FOR 1939

Area	Husband's Income $600–$999[a]		All Incomes	
	Children under 10		Children under 10	
	Without	With	Without	With
Metropolitan Areas				
Total	29.6	12.0	21.8	8.0
Nonwhite	36.5	21.5	38.2	20.1
Urban: 25,000–100,000				
Total	34.3	15.9	24.9	11.0
Nonwhite	54.0	....	52.1	39.8
Urban: 2,500–25,000				
Total	31.6	15.0	24.4	11.5
Nonwhite	44.9	29.1	50.0	37.8
Rural Nonfarm				
Total	21.2	8.8	18.9	8.6
Nonwhite	23.0	16.4	33.2	22.8

Source: Stanley Lebergott, "Population Change and the Supply of Labor," in *Demographic and Economic Change in Developed Countries*, National Bureau of Economic Research (Princeton: Princeton University Press, 1958), p. 397.

[a] The group of husband-wife families where the husband earned $600–$999 and the wife was 35–44 years of age is the modal income-age group among all nonwhite husband-wife families.

TABLE 40

LABOR FORCE PARTICIPATION RATES FOR URBAN AND RURAL NONFARM MARRIED WOMEN, HUSBAND PRESENT, BY INCOME OF HUSBAND (YEAR PRECEDING), COLOR, PRESENCE AND AGE OF CHILDREN

COMBINED 1959, 1960, 1961 (IN MARCH OF EACH YEAR)

Income Group	Color, Presence and Age of Children							
	Total		No Children under 18		Children 6-17 only		Children under 6	
	White	Non-white	White	Non-white	White	Non-white	White	Non-white
Total	30.4	44.3	35.4	52.7	39.4	54.5	17.5	30.7
Under $1,000	33.1	48.9	28.9	50.2	53.9	64.6	32.3	35.3
$1,000-$1,999	28.3	44.2	26.4	45.9	49.2	51.6	24.6	38.6
$2,000-$2,999	33.8	43.1	34.0	57.5	49.3	53.2	24.5	26.7
$3,000-$4,999	36.0	44.6	43.5	55.7	47.0	53.3	21.5	30.9
$5,000-$6,999	30.1	43.8	40.0	52.0	39.2	55.6	16.0	31.1
$7,000—over	22.2	32.3	30.1	[a]	28.2	[a]	10.7	[a]

Source: Unpublished data from the U.S. Department of Labor, Bureau of Labor Statistics, "Special Labor Force Reports," Nos. 7, 13, and 20. I am indebted to Harold Goldstein of the Bureau of Labor Statistics for this material.

[a] The number of observations are less than the minimum required for sampling reliability.

TABLE 41

EMPLOYMENT STATUS IN 1958 OF WIVES, HUSBAND PRESENT, BY COLOR AND BY INCOME OF HUSBAND

Wives with Some Employment in 1958	Total	Income of Husband for 1958					
		Less than $2,000	$2,000-2,999	$3,000-3,999	$4,000-4,999	$5,000-5,999	$6,000 and over
Whites:							
Number	23,089	3,925	2,309	3,002	3,925	3,694	6,234
Employment rate	40.1	42.5	48.2	46.3	44.8	37.6	31.2
Nonwhites:							
Number	1,879	714	319	357	282	132	75
Employment rate	59.4	65.7	63.0	50.1	55.3	50.1	60.0
Difference: NW − W	19.3	23.2	14.8	3.8	10.5	12.5	28.8

Source: Based on Table 11, p. 30 in *The Structure of Family Incomes* (labor force participation of family members in relation to income and employment status of family heads, families in the United States, March, 1959), Consumption Research Project, Department of Economics, University of Chicago.

TABLE 42

PER CENT FEMALE OF EMPLOYEES IN MAJOR INDUSTRIES: THE BASIS FOR THE MEASURE OF THE INDUSTRIAL STRUCTURE, "IND," OF THE SMA IN 1950

Male Demanders	% Female	Female Demanders	% Female
1. Mining	2.4	1. Entertainment and recreation	25.3
2. Construction	2.7	2. Public administration	25.9
3. Agriculture, forest., fish.	8.5	3. Wholesale and retail	33.8
4. Business and repair service	12.8	4. Industry not reported	34.2
5. Transportation and communication	15.4	5. Non-durable manufacturing	35.5
6. Durable manufacturing	15.9	6. Finance, insurance, real estate	40.7
		7. Professional and related	59.1
		8. Personal service	66.8

Source: The selection of industries to represent the demand for female labor is based on Table 130 from the *1950 Census of Population*, Vol. II: *Characteristics of the Population, Part 1, U.S. Summary*, pp. 283–84.

APPENDIX C

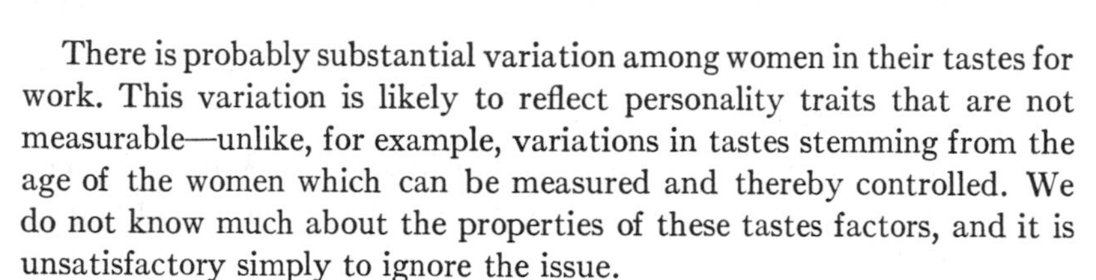

Changes in Attitudes and Tastes-for-Work in the Study of Labor Force Participation of Married Women

There is probably substantial variation among women in their tastes for work. This variation is likely to reflect personality traits that are not measurable—unlike, for example, variations in tastes stemming from the age of the women which can be measured and thereby controlled. We do not know much about the properties of these tastes factors, and it is unsatisfactory simply to ignore the issue.

The problem may be serious. As an example, we might have observations on the earnings abilities and the labor supply of individual wives and wish to determine the relation between these two variables. Will a positive relation imply that the higher earnings ability "causes" a greater offering of market labor? Or is a positive correlation spurious and actually attributable to a "tastes-for-market-work" variable that is positively related to both earnings and labor supply? If so, then in the extreme case of a true zero correlation between earnings and work, we would be incorrect in predicting an increase in work by wives over time in response to rises in wage rates offered to them, unless we knew whether tastes changed.

Undoubtedly this is too extreme. In the first place, it is not a certainty that tastes for market work and wage rates are positively related. We can imagine cases of individuals who have a strong distaste for work and who then strive to acquire a high wage that permits them to work relatively little and still earn an acceptable income. Among wives, however, we would expect the amount of market work, earnings ability (or wage rates), and tastes for market work, all to be positively correlated. There exists, then, the danger of obtaining biased estimates of the effect of wages on work when we do not control for the tastes variable.

Direct measures of tastes for market work, by such devices as gathering historical accounts of customs and conventions or by questioning the subjects about their attitudes, involve several problems. One is that the answers from these methods will in part reflect and be based on other variables in the model. For example, assume we have a model to explain work by wives that includes two independent variables, the wife's wage rate and her tastes for work. If the empirical variable used for the wage rate is a weak proxy for the true wage, then it may turn out that the empirical construct for tastes for work (like the wife's stated atitude toward working) will pick up some of the effect of the true wage rate, and the wage rate coefficient will be understated. The closer the relation between the two variables, the more serious becomes the problem of collinearity. Now, if the empirical variable for the wage perfectly represented the appropriate theoretical concept, the addition of a variable for tastes should have only some net effect that would not disturb the measure for the effect of wages on labor supplied. Unfortunately, we always work with proxy variables, and the disturbance might be serious.

A second problem is that attempts to include tastes often involve arbitrary measures—the asking of one question or another—that appear to be more ambiguous than are measures for income or age, for example. Even the manner in which the question is asked is likely to alter the answer. Clearly, then, there are pronounced difficulties in making comparisons among various studies.

The final problem is the lack of a firm theoretical footing for handling "attitudes" and the like. But since this issue lies in the field of psychology, I should add that any "lack" of a theoretical footing may be my own shortcoming.

One way to cope with the problem of tastes is to aggregate over individual observations. A reduction in variations in tastes will doubtless result from aggregation, since the extreme plus and minus values will tend to cancel each other. Furthermore, tastes will not vary much across groups of women if the basis of aggregation, itself, does not act as a proxy for tastes variation. Cross-section observations of large metropolitan areas in the United States should satisfy this condition. The type of variations in tastes owing to different historical points in time is obviously removed, and an area basis should be fairly neutral with regard to tastes. It is difficult to see why, for example, wives in New York, Los Angeles, and Chicago should be different, on the average, in their tastes for work. It may be, however, that variations in the religious or ethnic composition of populations across areas represent tastes differences. Here, the issues enter the realm of sociology, and except for the distinction between whites and nonwhites these characteristics are not analyzed in this study.

Aggregations that refer to different time periods are another matter. The claim is often made that over time "society's" and/or wives' tastes have grown more favorable to market work. Simply reciting the following list of events in this century suggests support for this view: the Progressive movement around the first decade that included feminist reforms, the incentives—partly social and political—to female employment during two world wars, and the heightened emancipation of women alleged to have occurred in the decade of the 1920's. Other less dramatic events could be cited. There are also some that have had opposite effects, however, such as laws restricting employment of women and the movement to the suburbs, to name two.

In any event, the task of separating the economic component that is involved and then of evaluating the remaining, change-in-tastes component is overwhelming. For example, even if we had evidence in the form, say, of a time series of Gallup polls on wives' attitudes toward work, we would not know whether or not this merely reflected the known more favorable economic incentives offered to women who chose to work. Just as in a cross-section we would expect women who report favorable attitudes toward work to be, on the average, those who can get or have "good" jobs, so the time series trend of "better" jobs available would account for some of the changing attitudes. The interesting and difficult question remains: What changes in attitudes and tastes are independent and causal in their effects on work by married women?

APPENDIX D

Measures of Labor Supply for Nonwhite and White Wives

The claim made in the text was that the common measure of labor force participation rates exaggerate the number of hours worked by nonwhite wives relative to white wives. Some direct evidence on this point is given with data from the 1-in-1,000 sample of the 1960 Census (see pp. 101–2 and Table 30). This appendix offers more support for this claim with evidence from several miscellaneous sources.

The published figures on full- and part-time work status among working females suggest the exaggeration noted above. During the period, 1955 to 1960, the proportion of employed females who were full-time workers ranged between 72 and 77 per cent for white females and 62 to 66 per cent for nonwhite females.[1]

Although a classification by marital status is not regularly published, a special tabulation from the 1959 Current Population Survey indicates that the difference in proportions for wives would be at least as large.[2] Using somewhat different categories of work status this tabulation shows that although 59 per cent of nonwhite wives and 40 per cent of white wives worked in 1958, 25 per cent of the nonwhite and 35 per cent of the white group of working wives were full-time and full-year workers. If it is assumed that all full-time workers worked 40 hours a week and part-time workers 20 hours, then white wives would have averaged 10.8 hours worked each week and nonwhite wives 14.8 hours. Using an hours-worked measure the rates for the two color groups are 27 per cent for white wives, 37 per cent for nonwhite wives.[3] Instead of a difference of 48 per cent [(59–40/40)] in rates of employment we find a difference of 37 per cent [(37–27/27)] in hours-worked rates.

[1] Robert L. Stein and Jane L. Meredith, "Growth and Characteristics of the Part-Time Labor Force," Special Labor Force Report, No. 10, U.S. Department of Labor, Bureau of Labor Statistics, p. A-4 of the reprint.

[2] *The Structure of Family Income*, p. 87, Table 38.

[3] For all white wives 14 per cent worked full-time, 26 per cent part-time, so $[(.14)(40) + (.26)(20)]/40 = 10.8/40 = 27\%$. For all nonwhite wives we have: $[(.15)(40)] + [(.44)(20)]/40 = 14.8/40 = 37\%$.

One direct estimate of the difference in hours worked per year by white and nonwhite wives is given in a paper by Morgan and David.[4] The participation rates they reported for the entire year of 1959 for white and nonwhite wives were 37 and 50 per cent, respectively; the average hours worked during 1959 by working wives were 1,375 and 1,097 hours for whites and nonwhites, respectively. Combining the figures for rate and hours worked gives a labor supply measure based on average hours worked per year out of 2,000 working hours (a 40-hour week times a 50-week year). These rates are 25 per cent for white wives and 27 percent for nonwhites.[5] The original difference of 13 percentage points in labor force participation rates is reduced to only 2 percentage points when hours are taken into account.

The same paper gave estimates standardized "as if the two populations were identical on many other characteristics such as education, occupation, age, etc." Standardized estimates of proportions of wives who worked in 1959 were .44 for nonwhite wives and .37 for white wives; for hours worked 1,076 and 1,378, respectively.[6] The product of the rates and hours gives an average hours-worked-per year. In this case we find white wives working more! They average 510 hours compared with 473 hours for nonwhite wives.

[4] James N. Morgan and Martin David, "Race, Economic Attitudes, and Behavior," 1962 *Proceedings of the Social Statistics Section of the American Statistical Association*, p. 10, Table 6.

[5] For white wives: [(.37)(1,375)]/2,000 = 25%. For nonwhite wives: [(.50)(1,097)]/2,000 = 27%.

[6] For these calculations I used a corrected table of figures kindly given to me by Martin David. The corrections are made on Table 6 of the original article.

APPENDIX E

Computational Procedures for Tables 23 and 24 Regarding Earnings Data and a Time-Series Prediction Based on Cross-Section Regression Results

I. Table 23 shows the percentage increase in median wage and salary incomes of year-round, full-time workers by sex and color, 1939–1957.

A. The derivation begins with Table 43, which is self-explanatory except for point B which follows.

B. Computation of "adjusted earnings" of nonwhite females.

A measure of the earnings of nonwhite females which included an estimate of income-in-kind from employment in domestic service was calculated. These measures are based on the data in Tables 44 and 45 below.

About 60 per cent of nonwhite females who worked were domestic servants in 1940.[1] Stigler reported that about one-third of all domestic servants in 1940 received food and lodging from their employers,[2] and if we apply this percentage to nonwhites we arrive at column (1) in Table 44. The dollar value of the income-in-kind received by domestics who "lived in" was $140 for this year according to Stigler.[3] Assume that this applies to nonwhites and that nonwhite domestic servants who did not "live in" received $70 of income-in-kind in 1939. This gives us column (3) in Table 44. The median money income of nonwhite females who worked year around was $327, and the median money income of all female domestic servants in 1939 (half of whom were nonwhite) was $339 for year-around workers.[4] Based on these figures I drew up column (2) showing "estimated money income" for the three types of nonwhite working females. The weighted average of these estimates is $320. The estimates were based in part on their weighted average being similar to the actual average which

[1] Stigler, *Trends in Employment in the Service Industry*, p. 101.

[2] Stigler, *Domestic Servants in the United States, 1900–1940*, p. 16.

[3] Stigler, *Trends in Employment in the Service Industry*, p. 94.

[4] Herman P. Miller, *Income of the American People*, (New York: John Wiley and Sons, 1955) p. 192.

is $327. Column (4) in Table 44 is simply the sum of columns (2) and (3). The weighted average of the "adjusted total income" in column (4) is $376, and this is the amount entered in Table 43.

Table 45 gives the same set of figures for 1957 as Table 44 did for 1939, and it is derived in a similar manner. By 1960, 37 per cent of nonwhite

TABLE 43

WAGE AND SALARY INCOMES OF YEAR-ROUND, FULL-TIME WORKERS (DEFLATED INCOMES IN PARENTHESES) FOR 1939 AND 1957 BY RACE AND SEX

Year	White Males	White Females	Nonwhite Males	Nonwhite Females
1939	$1,419[a] (2,881)[b]	$ 863 (1,752)	$ 639 (1,297)	$ 327 (664)
1957	4,950 (4,702)	3,107 (2,952)	3,107 (2,980)	1,866 (1,773)
1939 (adjusted)[c]	....	....	....	376 (763)
1957 (adjusted)[c]	....	....	....	1,917 (1,821)

[a] Source: "Economic Situation of Negroes in the United States," p. 16.

[b] The Personal Consumption Expenditure Series was used for deflating the dollar figures: 1954 = 100. Source: *Business Statistics,* 1959 Edition, p.p 2–3, and Selma F. Goldsmith, "Size Distribution of Personal Income, 1956–1959," *Survey of Current Business,* April, 1960, p. 9.

[c] Source: Explained under part B, pp. 136–38.

TABLE 44

INCOME IN 1939 OF NONWHITE FEMALES WHO WERE YEAR-ROUND WORKERS

Occupation	Per Cent of Total (1)	Money Income (Estimated) (2)	Income-in-kind (3)	Adjusted Total Income (4)
Domestics who "lived in"	20	$200	$140	$340
Domestics who did not "live in"	40	300	70	370
Not domestic servants	40	400	0	400

females who worked were domestic servants.[5] I assumed that only one-sixth "lived in." Column (2) is constructed with two pieces of information. First, the median salary for year-round domestic servants in 1960 was $1,133 when half the members of this occupation were white.[6] Considering that incomes were lower in 1957 and were lower for nonwhites than for whites, I estimated the full-time earnings for nonwhite domestic servants in 1957 to be $844. This amount underlies the first two figures in

[5] "The Economic Situation of Negroes in the United States," p. 13.

[6] *Ibid.,* p. 15.

column (2). Second, the amount of income earned by nonwhite females who worked the year-round in 1957 was $1,866.[7] On the basis of this amount we can derive the third figure in column (2) so that the weighted average of all three figures in the column is $1,864. (This is to match the actual amount of $1,866.) In column (3) conservative estimates are made for income-in-kind to avoid overstating nonwhite incomes in 1957.

II. Derivation of Table 24 that predicts time series labor force participation rates using cross-sectional regression results.

A. The figures in parentheses in Table 43 were subtracted to get dollar changes from 1939 to 1957. These were applied to the respective regression coefficients in lines 6 of Table 11 and 1 of Table 19. The regional dummy variable coefficient was ignored since population shifts from the South

TABLE 45

INCOME IN 1957 OF NONWHITE FEMALES WHO WERE YEAR-ROUND WORKERS

Occupation	Per Cent of Total (1)	Money Income (Estimated) (2)	Income-in-Kind (3)	Adjusted Total Income (4)
Domestics who "lived in"..........	7	$ 600	$250	$ 850
Domestics who did not "live in"....	30	900	125	1,025
Not domestic servants.............	63	2,460	0	2,460

to the North have not been so great as to seriously alter the results. For whites we have: (1.09) (12.00) – (.16) (18.21) = 10, or 10 percentage points in labor force participation rates. For nonwhites: (2.88) (11.09) – (1.48) (16.83) = 7. For nonwhites, adjusted: (2.88) (10.58) – (1.48) (16.83) = 5.6.

B. From Table 10 in the text I estimated the "actual change" in labor force participation rates. Using the comparison between the 1950 census rates and the 1950 Current Population Survey rates as a guide, the 1940 rates were adjusted to read 14 per cent for white wives, 30 per cent for nonwhite wives. Subtracting these approximations from the 1957 Current Population rates, 29 per cent and 40 per cent, respectively, gives the "actual change" figures in the first column of Table 24.

[7] Current Population Reports, Series P-60, No. 37, January 17, 1962.

APPENDIX F

Age at Marriage and the Educational Attainment of the Wife

The purpose of this appendix is to present the tests of the contention made in the text that the relation between the educational attainment of the wife and her age at marriage is positive, if the cohort of the wife is held constant. In other words, for wives of a given age, the greater their educational attainment is, the older they were when they married. It then follows that wives of a given age will tend to be married fewer years the more years of schooling they have completed. For this reason years worked while married for wives of given ages would be negatively related to education since the latter variable is negatively related to years married.

The observed relation between age at marriage and education of the wife will be affected by two pronounced secular trends—increasing years of schooling and earlier marriages. It is, therefore, essential to control for the age-at-birth, or cohort, of the wife to isolate the relation between age at marriage and education. I have discussed elsewhere the existing studies on this relation and how they compare with the empirical work I present.[1]

In this appendix I will simply show the results of tests I have made with the Growth of American Families (GAF) data. This should be sufficient in this context since it is only with these data that I have examined the determinants of years worked by the wife (as one application of the economic model of the labor supply of the wife).

The GAF study is well-suited for an examination of the subject matter of this appendix. It included information on age of wife, age at first marriage, and educational attainment. I restricted the sample to nonfarm residents without "missing data." The sample size was 2,265. For each of the 22 single-year age groups the average age at first marriage was computed for 10 educational classes. The two largest cohort groups, for ages 28 and 32, are shown in Table 46 along with the 20-year-olds, who

[1] Glen G. Cain, "A Note on the Interrelations of Age at Marriage, Education, and Work of the Wife: An Application of Cohort Analysis," University of Wisconsin, Social Systems Research Institute, Workshop on the Economic Behavior of Households: Paper 6502, June, 1965.

were the largest group among the youngest wives, aged 18–21. Age at marriage rises with education over most of the range. The age groups are representative although the numbers in many of the cells are so few that a different means of presenting the data is necessary. I turn next to a summary of the relationship between age at marriage, *M*, and education of the wife, *E*, for all ages by means of regression analysis.

We should remember that relatively few wives have less than a seventh or eighth grade education in a sample such as that used above. Let us

TABLE 46

AVERAGE AGE AT FIRST MARRIAGE BY EDUCATION OF WIFE FOR SELECTED AGE GROUPS (NUMBER OF OBSERVATIONS IN PARENTHESES)

COHORT GROUP	YEARS OF SCHOOLING COMPLETED[a]								
	1–4	5–6	7	8	9–11	12	13–15	16	Over 16
Aged 20 (71)	...... (0)	18.0 (1)	16.5 (2)	17.0 (1)	17.1 (24)	18.1 (38)	19.0 (5)	...... (0)	...... (0)
Aged 28 (161)	18.0 (1)	18.0 (2)	17.8 (6)	19.0 (7)	18.5 (40)	20.1 (82)	21.0 (13)	24.0 (5)	24.8 (5)
Aged 32 (154)	20.8 (4)	18.0 (3)	18.5 (4)	20.0 (12)	20.3 (32)	22.3 (80)	21.5 (14)	24.0 (3)	28.5 (2)

Source: Special tabulation of Growth of American Families (GAF) data.

[a] No wives in these age groups had less than 1 year's schooling, so there is no column for "Less than 1 year's schooling."

include this dimension of the problem and investigate the relation between *M* and *E* that is most typical; that is, one weighted by the number of observations found in the various classifications. We can use regression analysis to get an over-all measure. Assume that *M* and *E* are characterized by some curvilinear (U-shaped) relation.[2] Specifically we seek the best fitting quadratic curve relating *M* to *E* and E^2. Then, with this curve, what is the value of *E* where *M* is a minimum? Table 47 shows the results of regressing *M* on *E*, E^2, and 10 dummy variables for *A*, the

[2] Although a regression model is used, I do not claim that *E* "causes" *M*. It is more appropriate to think of *M* and *E* possessing a joint probability distribution—given other variables—where, in the model above, the other variable is the cohort of the wife. If the U-shaped relation between *M* and *E* is at all accurate, then, the designation of *M* as the dependent variable is reasonable. For each value of *E* there corresponds a single most likely value of *M;* thus, we seek to determine the value of *M* given values of *E* and *A* the age of the wife. I am indebted to Guy Orcutt for pointing out this interpretation of a regression framework in this context.

current age of the wife.[3] The last line in Table 47 shows a regression with an additional variable representing the wife's "potential earnings" in the job market. This line is referred to later.

The regressions on lines 1 and 2 do not include the dummy variables for age and give very poor fits. In line 2 age at marriage is a minimum at 5.8 years of education.[4] In line 3 the age of marriage, holding current age of the wife constant, is a minimum at 1.8 years of education. Since the mean value of years of schooling completed for the wives in the sample is 11.3

TABLE 47

RELATION OF AGE AT MARRIAGE AND EDUCATION WITH CONTROL OVER THE AGE OF WIFE[a]

LINE	R^2 [b]	Independent Variable (Standard Errors in Parentheses)				
		Constant	Education in Years	Education Squared in Years	10 Age Dummies	Wife's Earning Capacity
1......	.054	16.46 (.35)	.341 (.030)	....	....	....
2......	.066	20.30 (.79)	−.417 (.143)	.036 (.007)	....	....
3......	.195	20.16 (.75)	−.074 (.134)	.020 (.006)	Positive[c]	....
4......	.192	18.01 (.37)	.356 (.028)	....	Positive[c]	....
5......	.208	19.12 (.76)	−.078 (.133)	.016 (.006)	Positive[c]	.097 (.016)

Source: Growth of American Families survey, 2,265 observations.

[a] Dependent variable: Age of wife at marriage (mean = 20.32, standard deviation = 3.38).

[b] The multiple correlation, R^2, is corrected for degrees of freedom.

[c] Age was positively related to age-at-marriage, and the set of dummy variables for age were all significant on the basis of an *F*-ratio test.

(with a standard deviation of 2.3), it is clear that this curve relating *M* and *E* is positive over almost the entire range of education. Line 4 shows that a linear relation for *E* does almost as well as the quadratic form if the age-of-wife variables are included.

AN INTERPRETATION OF THE RESULTS

Females with the *least* education tend to marry at relatively older ages. The explanation that these women are less attractive as marriage partners[5] seems reasonable, especially when applied to those with less

[3] The age groups are paired as follows: 18–19, 20–21, . . . , 36–37, with the eleventh age group, 38–39, being the omitted group in the regressions.

[4] The first derivative of the regression equation is taken, $\partial M/\partial E$, yielding a first order term for education that is solved for when the first derivative is set equal to zero.

[5] See, for example, Paul C. Glick, *American Families* (New York: John Wiley and Sons, 1957), p. 115.

than 4 or 5 years of schooling. Past this minimal level of education, however, the relation between education and age at marriage would be expected to be positive if we apply the economic theory of "occupational choice" to the marriage decision. The application is clearest for females who have attended college. We can think of these females as having chosen for a period of years the "occupation" of student in preference to that of housewife, if they have the means and desires to continue schooling. For females with 12 years of schooling or less (but more than, say, 4 years), we can similarly think of the "occupation" of housewife being preferred to that of market workers for those non-student women with a low education and a consequent comparative disadvantage in the job market. Past some minimum level of education, then, more years of schooling represent improved job and educational opportunities that serve as an alternative to the occupation of housewife; below this minimal level, marriage may be as difficult to secure as an acceptable job.

Thus, in line 5 of Table 47 we see that the wife's potential market earnings bears a significant positive relation to her age at marriage, holding the other variables constant.[6] This result is consistent with the "occupational choice" theory of marriage, but further testing would be needed to determine whether job skills yielding high earnings are merely a result of a late marriage rather than a cause, which is implied by the "dependent-independent" dichotomy among variables in the regression model.

[6] See p. 92 for the definition and source of "potential market earnings."

APPENDIX G

The Relationship between Nonwhite Housing and Labor Force Participation of Nonwhite Wives

In this appendix, I discuss the relation of housing expenditures to the labor force participation of married women, with special reference to nonwhite wives. Essentially, three points are made. (1) There is a positive relation between the amount of housing purchased and the amount of the wife's homework. A corollary is an inverse relation between the amount of housing and market work by the wife. (2) Nonwhites obtain less housing than whites, holding income constant, and appear to pay more for equivalent housing. This point is economically interesting as an explanation for the higher labor force participation rates of nonwhite wives if some factor other than "tastes" is shown to underlie the color difference in housing purchases and work choices. (3) Discrimination in the housing market is a factor that would explain these observed differences.

(1) The point of departure is the model of the text in which the family unit divides its consumption among three broad categories of goods: market goods, home goods, and leisure. In the production of these goods the wife, more than any other family member, straddles the boundary between home and market. Therefore, the substitution between home production and market production is greater (more elastic) for the wife.

Market goods will be substitutable, neutral, or complementary with respect to home goods. Restaurant meals, for example, are clearly a substitute. The home or rental unit itself is a complement. Consider, as an illustration, the stimulus to homework of a large home in a pleasant neighborhood compared with a small apartment in a shabby neighborhood.

Among individual families the positive relation of the amount of housing purchased to the wife's homework (and the negative relation to the wife's market work) is of little interest. The relation will mostly reflect a number of characteristics already under investigation (like income) or the variations in consumers' tastes for housing. As the next point brings out, however, there are striking differences in housing between whites and nonwhites that are not fully accounted for by such customary variables as income and family size. It is this difference between the two color groups, as aggregates and in conjunction with the model of discrimination, that contributes to an explanation of the color differences in labor force participation.

(2) In the absence of a strict quantity measure of housing we can make use of a quality measure for the "amount" of housing; namely, the per cent of renter-occupied dwelling units that are substandard (census definition). Table 48 from the report of the Commission on Race and Housing by Davis McEntire shows that nonwhites buy less housing than whites

TABLE 48

PER CENT OF RENTER-OCCUPIED DWELLING UNITS STANDARD BY INCOME AND COLOR OF OCCUPANTS FOR SELECTED SMA'S IN 1950

SMA and Color	Total	Income of Primary Families and Individuals			
		Up to $2,000	$2,000–2,999	$4,000–4,999	$7,000 and Over
Los Angeles W.....	88.2	79.0	87.4	94.5	98.0
NW...	73.8	65.8	75.3	85.1	87.9
Birmingham W.....	56.7	39.6	45.3	73.8	87.7
NW...	7.0	7.7	5.2	7.9	21.4

Source: Davis McEntire, *Residence and Race* (Berkeley and Los Angeles: University of California Press, 1960), p. 136, Table 19.

at comparable incomes. In using the current, reported income figures in Table 48, I correct for the direction of bias of the appropriate permanent income concept by comparing each nonwhite income class to the next lower white income class. The assumption is that whites in a given income bracket have the same permanent or normal income as the nonwhites in the next higher current income bracket.[1] This permits three income-group comparisons, and for all eight cities shown in McEntire's tables, nonwhites had a higher per cent of substandard dwellings for each of the 24 comparisons. The two cities listed above provide the narrowest and widest color differences. Note that the last three breaks in income classes

[1] Among nonwhites and whites who have the same current income, the presumption is that the whites will have higher normal incomes. Since housing expenditures are likely to be geared to the normal income of the family, the amount of housing bought—or, say, the ratio of housing expenditures to current income—will be biased upward for whites relative to nonwhites.

McEntire lists strengthen the point that nonwhites buy less housing than do whites who have similar incomes, since white current incomes that are considerably lower than nonwhite current incomes are compared on the basis that they represent similar normal or permanent incomes.

Furthermore, nonwhites appear to pay more for equivalent housing, or, as the tables are arranged, to get less housing than whites within the same rent categories. Holding rent constant, McEntire reports that nonwhites obtained fewer standard dwellings than whites at every level of rent (five rent classes) for all eight standard metropolitan areas, except for one cell out of the 40.[2] The differentials are much wider in the South

TABLE 49

SELECTED STATISTICS FOR RENTER HOUSEHOLDS IN CHICAGO FOR 1956

	Per Cent of Renter Households Occupying Substandard Dwellings	Median Gross Monthly Rental	Median Family Income
White	17	$78	$5,910
Nonwhite	35	76	4,192

Source: Beverly Duncan and Philip M. Hauser, *Housing a Metropolis—Chicago* (Glencoe: The Free Press, 1960), pp. 184–88.

than in the North or West, except for Chicago and St. Louis. The one-sided picture of a rent-and-quality comparison is somewhat modified by a quantity variable. With rent held constant, whites have a larger number of rooms in 38 cases, nonwhites have more in 30, and the number is equal in four.[3]

A closer check on these and other important variables is provided in the study of the Chicago housing market in 1956 by Beverly Duncan and Philip Hauser.[4] The over-all comparison between whites and nonwhites is given in Table 49.

Table 6–13 in Duncan and Hauser shows that nonwhites have a

[2] Davis McEntire, *Residence and Race* (Berkeley and Los Angeles: University of California Press, 1960), p. 150, Table 25.

[3] Although the entire discussion in this section has been in terms of rental dwelling units, the conclusions would be roughly the same for owner-occupied houses. To give McEntire's data on house dwellings would only duplicate what has been found for rental units. See McEntire, *op. cit.*, p. 378, Table A-12.

[4] Beverly Duncan and Philip M. Hauser, *Housing a Metropolis—Chicago* (Glencoe: The Free Press, 1960).

higher percentage of substandard housing than whites at each of eleven rent brackets. When size of apartment as well as rent is held constant, the proportion of substandard dwellings remains consistently higher for nonwhites.[5] In another comparison when white and nonwhite families of the same size, type, and income are compared, the proportion of substandard dwellings is again consistently higher for nonwhites.[6] Since the nonwhites appear to pay higher rents than whites at comparable incomes (this is implicit in Table 49), a control by rent would reduce the quality differential by less than does income. That is, at the same income nonwhites have poorer housing even though they appear to be paying higher rents. So, at the same level of rent payments they would be receiving housing that compares even more unfavorably with that received by whites, where family type and size are controlled.

(3) The point made in the text concerning the pronounced inferiority of nonwhite housing seems firmly supported by the data shown above. Whether nonwhites pay more for equivalent housing is more difficult to establish. On a more theoretical level, the case for discrimination in housing—the existence of a "tax" on Negro housing—is readily suggested by a straightforward application of the model developed by Gary Becker of discrimination in the labor market.[7]

Briefly, the housing market model assumes that a white society, *W*, has an abundance of property it exports to a nonwhite society, *N*, which has an abundance of tenants. If members of *W* have tastes for discrimination against *N*, this will be expressed in the willingness of *W* property owners to forfeit money (in this case, rental) income to avoid contact with *N* tenants. The result is that in equilibrium *W* property owners would earn less property income and *N* tenants would pay higher rents than if no discrimination existed.

If we assume that *W* property owners do not discriminate but *W* tenants do, then segregation but not discrimination results, as long as perfect competition prevails and we consider *W* and *N* tenants as perfect substitutes (to property owners). But both of the qualifying conditions are dubious assumptions.

[5] *Ibid.*, pp. 193–96.

[6] *Ibid.*, pp. 196 ff. See Table 6–15. Family type is a variable that offers some control over the quality of the tenant. There are four family types used by the authors: (1) atypical—families who share their dwellings with nonrelatives and/or where the spouse of the family head is absent; (2) primary individual, living alone; (3) primary individual, living with nonrelatives; (4) normal (where all members living together are related).

[7] Gary S. Becker, *The Economics of Discrimination* (Chicago: University of Chicago Press, 1957).

Perfect competition is untenable because of the collective efforts and practices of neighborhood organizations, realtor organizations, and neighborhood savings and loan associations that restrict "entry" by nonwhites to housing markets in ways analogous to certain trade unions' restrictions on entry to the labor market. Another analogy with the labor market is that between occupational licensing and neighborhood zoning regulations. The existence of all these impediments to a free market in housing for Negroes is amply documented in the two volumes of the Commission on Race and Housing.[8] Another impediment is rent controls, which are in effect in New York, where about 5 per cent of nonwhites live.[9] Outside of New York, however, rent controls were important for only a brief period in the 1940's.

The assumption that *W* and *N* tenants are perfect substitutes to property owners may also be inappropriate. If *N* tenants are poorer financial risks or are believed to be less desirable tenants in other "real" respects, then premiums on the rents charged them become "economic" rather than "discriminatory." From the standpoint of the labor force participation model, however, it does not matter what exogenous factor (tastes for discrimination against nonwhites, their characteristics of riskiness, or the market disadvantage many have as recent in-migrants) is the source of the "tax" on their housing expenditure, although the term "tax" becomes inappropriate. The outcome would still be higher prices of housing for nonwhites, and a consequent disincentive to homework and an encouragement to market work.

[8] McEntire, *op. cit.*, and *Studies in Housing and Minority Groups*, eds. Nathan Glazer and Davis McEntire (Berkeley and Los Angeles: University of California Press, 1960).

[9] See Becker, *op. cit.*, p. 60.

APPENDIX H

An Attempted Simultaneous System

In chapter 2 there is a discussion of the application of a regression model to cross-section aggregative data. The validity of the single equation model used with SMA aggregations rests on the assumption that the dependent variable is affected by the independent variables of the system but does not affect them. This assumption is probably shakiest with regard to the wage variable. If we look, therefore, upon the labor force participation rate of wives and the female wage rate variable as mutually interdependent, we can set up the group of just-identified systems of simultaneous equations shown in Table 50. The innovation required is the use of an industrial structure variable, *Ind*, as an exogenous (or predetermined) measure of the level of demand conditions. (The relation is expected to be negative since *Ind* measures the proportion of the labor force in male-demanding industries in the SMA. See Table 42.)

Consider the following structural equations. Equation (1) expresses the supply of labor of married women, M^S, as a function of husband's income, Y, the female wage rate, W, the region, R (North = 0; South = 1), and the unemployment experience of males, U. Equation (2) expresses the demand for work of wives as a function of W, R, U and the industrial structure in the SMA. Equation (3) expresses the equilibrium condition that the supply of labor equals the demand for labor.

$$M^S = F_S\,(Y, W, R, U) \qquad (1)$$

$$M^D = F_D\,(Ind, W, R, U) \qquad (2)$$

$$M^S = M^D = M \qquad (3)$$

Express (1) in the following form:

$$M = b_{11}\,Y + b_{12}\,W + b_{13}\,R + b_{14}\,U + V_1 \qquad (4)$$

Express (2) in terms of W:

$$W = b_{21}\,(Ind) + B_{22}\,M + b_{23}\,R + b_{24}\,U + V_2 \qquad (5)$$

Variations of these equations are shown in Table 50, where the lower-case letters for the variables are defined as they were throughout this book; see Appendix A for the glossary of symbols and Table 37 for their sources.

The solutions to the equations, also shown in Table 50, are derived by the method of indirect least-squares.[1] The derivation of the solution for the third system is shown at the end of this appendix, and all other solutions are obtained in a similar way.

The experiment must be judged a failure, even though the structural coefficients on y and w' are favorable to the hypothesis that the wage effect exceeds the income effect. Other results of the tests are inconsistent with the theory underlying the model. The positive sign on *ind* in the w' equation can be rationalized as reflecting the fact that the heavy industry cities are high wage rate areas, but the positive sign on m in the same equation must mean that *ind* simply does not adequately control for demand conditions. We can see from the solution to Model III (p. 150) that

TABLE 50

SIMULTANEOUS SYSTEMS AND THEIR STRUCTURAL COEFFICIENTS

I.	$m = b_{11}y + b_{12}w'$	$m = -1.94y + 4.10w'$
	$w' = b_{21}\,(ind) + b_{22}m$	$w' = .42\,(ind) + 1.72m$
II.	$m = b_{11}y + b_{12}w' + b_{13}r$	$m = -.68y + 2.51w' + 5.78r$
	$w' = b_{21}\,(ind) + b_{22}m + b_{23}r$	$w' = .11\,(ind) + .89m - 4.05$
III.	$m = b_{11}y + b_{12}w' + b_{13}r + b_{14}u'$	$m = -.59y + 2.65w' + 6.38r - .54u'$
	$w' = b_{21}\,(ind) + b_{22}m + b_{23}r + b_{24}u'$	$w' = .11\,(ind) + .92m - 4.10r - .44u'$

this critically wrong sign on m stems from the positive sign on y (see A_{11} in equation 3.4) in the reduced form equation where m is regressed on y, *ind*, r, and u'. In this equation *ind* does have the appropriate negative sign, but the positive sign on y indicates that y stands more as a proxy for a wage rate variable than it does as a proxy for the (negative) income effect. Again, *ind* does not carry out its assigned role.

It is likely that two variables in the system presented here are not defined with sufficient precision. First, *ind*, formerly used as an index of a "heavy" or "light" industrial structure, here works with industrial categories too broad to act alone as *the* demand variable. Secondly, m is at best a measure of the quantity of labor supplied, whereas in the equation determining w' a quality measure is also needed. Indeed, when I used a variable, m^*, defined as m times e (the median educational attainment of females in the SMA), the "incorrectness" of the coefficients on *ind* and m in the w' equation are reduced considerably. The new system solves out as:

$$m^* = -.40\,y + 3.89\,w' + 9.09\,r - .79\,u'$$

$$w' = .03\,(ind) + .35\,m^* - 2.74\,r - .20\,u'$$

[1] See J. Johnston, *Econometric Methods* (New York: McGraw-Hill, 1963), pp. 231–53.

It is clear that to pursue the estimation of coefficients in these and similar simultaneous systems would require another research project. Different specifications and different estimation methods to the two-equation systems is one path for future research; adding more equations to the systems is another.

Model III and Its Solution

$$m = b_{11}\, y + b_{12}\, w' + b_{13}\, r + b_{14}\, u' \tag{3.1}$$

$$w' = b_{21}\, ind + b_{22}\, m + b_{23}\, r + b_{24}\, u' \tag{3.2}$$

Simultaneous solution for m yields:

$$m = \frac{b_{11}}{Z} y + \frac{b_{12} b_{21}}{Z} ind + \frac{b_{12} b_{23} + b_{13}}{Z} r + \frac{b_{12} b_{24} + b_{14}}{Z} u' \tag{3.3}$$

where $Z = 1 - b_{12}\, b_{22}$.

Let A_{ij} stand for the coefficients of (3.3) that were determined by regression techniques:

$$m = A_{11}\, y + A_{12}\, ind + A_{13}\, r + A_{14}\, u' \tag{3.4}$$

$$= .41\, y - .20\, ind + 3.13\, r - .25\, u' \qquad R^2 = .50$$
$$(.16) \quad (.40) \quad (1.01) \quad (.17)$$

Simultaneous solution for w' yields:

$$w' = \frac{b_{21}}{Z} ind + \frac{b_{22} b_{11}}{Z} y + \frac{b_{22} b_{13} + b_{23}}{Z} r + \frac{b_{22} b_{14} + b_{24}}{Z} u' \tag{3.5}$$

$$w' = A_{21}\, ind + A_{22}\, y + A_{23}\, r + A_{24}\, u' \tag{3.6}$$

$$= -.08\, ind + .38\, y - 1.23\, r - .21\, u' \qquad R^2 = .57$$
$$(.03) \quad (.10) \quad (.60) \quad (.10)$$

then:

$$\underline{b_{12} = \frac{A_{12}}{A_{21}} = 2.645}, \qquad \underline{b_{22} = \frac{A_{22}}{A_{11}} = .918}$$

$$Z = -1.428$$

$$\underline{b_{11} = Z\, A_{11} = -.589}, \qquad \underline{b_{21} = Z\, A_{21} = .110}$$

$$b_{13} = Z\, A_{13} - b_{12}\, b_{23} \qquad b_{14} = Z\, A_{14} - b_{12}\, b_{24}$$

$$b_{23} = Z\, A_{23} - b_{22}\, b_{13} \qquad b_{24} = Z\, A_{24} - b_{22}\, b_{14}$$

$$b_{13} = Z\, A_{13} - b_{12}\, (Z\, A_{23} - b_{22}\, b_{13})$$

$$= Z\, A_{13} - b_{12}\, Z\, A_{23} + b_{12}\, b_{22}\, b_{13},$$

transposing

$$b_{13}(1 - b_{12} b_{22}) = Z A_{13} - b_{12} Z A_{23}$$

Since $1 - b_{12} b_{22} = Z$

we have:

$$b_{13} = A_{13} - b_{12} A_{23}$$

$$\underline{b_{13} = 6.381}$$

Similarly:

$$b_{23} = A_{23} - b_{22} A_{13}$$

$$\underline{b_{23} = -4.105}$$

$$b_{14} = A_{24} - b_{12} A_{24}$$

$$\underline{b_{14} = -.544}$$

$$b_{24} = A_{24} - b_{22} A_{14}$$

$$\underline{b_{24} = -.436}$$

APPENDIX J

The Relation between Unemployment Rates and the Labor Force Participation Rates of Secondary Workers

A number of regressions in the text, particularly those in the section of the book containing Tables 16, 17, and 18, indicated that unemployment in a city or an SMA was negatively related to the labor force participation of wives in the area. These tests used census data from three years, 1940, 1950, and 1960, made use of different measures of unemployment, and checked on biases in the coefficients by including a number of other variables. In this appendix I wish to examine briefly more evidence on the effect of unemployment by looking at other groups of "secondary workers." Wives are the most numerous among this imprecisely defined segment of the labor force; the remainder is comprised of older single women, older males, and teen-age workers (see footnote 16 on p. 62).

Four age groups were selected to represent secondary workers, excluding wives (see the list below). Labor force participation rates (LFPR) were computed for 60 SMA's in 1960 with a population over 250,000 and less than 10 per cent nonwhite. The rates are meant to reflect the participation of the white population. Plans to select a larger variety of groups and to conduct more extensive testing were made unnecessary by the publication of the research of Bowen and Finegan on this topic.[1] Their data, methods, and findings are similar to mine.

To determine the net (or partial) effect of unemployment, the basic model of labor supply was used. There is some control over the effects of income and wages, but not with the degree of specificity that was achieved with the study of married women. The measures used for income are: Y, the median income of the male head of the household in the SMA, and Y_n, the same measure for income from non-labor sources that was

[1] Their work examines the effect of unemployment on the labor force participation rates of five demographic groups: wives, teen-age girls and boys, older men, and prime-age men. Regressions were computed for the cross-sections of SMA's or cities from the census data of 1940, 1950, and 1960. Bowen and Finegan, "Labor Force Participation and Unemployment."

used for the 1960 regressions in the text (see Table 15 and Appendix A for a full definition). The proxy for the wage rate was as follows:

Age Group	The Variable for the Wage Rate of the Group
Single women, aged 55–59	Median income of females, 55–64
Single women, aged 18–19	Median income of females, 20–24
Males, 65 years and older	Median income of males, 65–74
Males, aged 14–19	Median income of males, 14–19

A regional variable was again used; 1 if a southern SMA, 0 if otherwise. Two demographic variables were used: A_{65}, the per cent of the population aged 65 and older, and A_m, the per cent of the population in the middle range, aged 18 to 64.

The principal unemployment rate used was U, the rate for the civilian labor force. A second rate, U_T, was computed in which the denominator was the total population eligible to be in the labor force. The reason for using this measure is discussed in the text, pages 67–69 and footnote 20.

It is unfortunate that the variables available for representing W and Y are so crude, but the purpose of the tests shown in Table 51 are simply to test the effect of unemployment and not to determine wage and income effects. The results of these regressions support the hypothesis about unemployment that the discouraging wage effect (or employment opportunity effect) overpowers the stimulus to work prompted by the decline in incomes. Generally, significantly negative effects of U and U_T appear for each group except for single females, aged 18 to 19. Here they are negative but not significant. The effects of W and Y are somewhat erratic, but where significant they usually possess the predicted sign. Constant terms have been omitted in the table.

TABLE 51

REGRESSION RESULTS OF THE EFFECTS OF UNEMPLOYMENT ON THE LABOR FORCE PARTICIPATION OF SELECTED GROUPS OF SECONDARY WORKERS FOR 60 SMA'S IN 1960

Dependent Variable: Labor Force Participation Rate (LFPR) of:	Line	Form	R^2	Independent Variable (Standard Errors in Parentheses): Y	Y_n	W	U	A_{65}	A_M	Net U_T Effect[a]	R^2 with U_T
I. Males, aged 65 and older[c]	1	A	.56	−0.17	−0.14	0.08	−1.72[b]	0.10	0.27	−2.93[b]	.55
				(0.09)	(0.42)	(0.09)	(0.24)	(0.22)	(0.23)	(0.41)	
	2	L	.56	−0.12	−0.06	0.08	−0.32[b]	−0.03	0.53	−0.30[b]	.56
				(0.16)	(0.08)	(0.10)	(0.05)	(0.06)	(0.46)	(0.04)	
II. Males, aged 14–19[c]	3	A	.41	0.13	1.17	6.31[b]	−1.19[b]	−0.45	−1.02[b]	−1.88[b]	.40
				(0.17)	(0.85)	(1.49)	(0.49)	(0.45)	(0.51)	(0.85)	
	4	L	.46	0.30[b]	0.13	1.19[b]	−0.19[b]	−0.07	−1.66[b]	−0.15[b]	.44
				(0.20)	(0.10)	(0.27)	(0.07)	(0.09)	(0.69)	(0.06)	
III. Single females, aged 18–19[c]	5	A	.44	0.22	−0.49	1.25[b]	−0.59	0.28	−1.01	−0.74	.43
				(0.19)	(0.95)	(0.24)	(0.56)	(0.54)	(0.55)	(0.97)	
	6	L	.36	0.24	−0.03	0.26[b]	−0.08	0.07	−0.97[b]	−0.06	.36
				(0.18)	(0.09)	(0.07)	(0.06)	(0.09)	(0.58)	(0.06)	
IV. Single females, aged 55–59[c]	7	A	.36	0.33	0.03	0.68[b]	−1.02[b]	0.35	−1.91[b]	−1.71	.35
				(0.24)	(1.00)	(0.33)	(0.59)	(0.55)	(0.57)	(1.00)	
	8	L	.35	0.45[b]	0.04	0.06	−0.12[b]	0.04	−1.73[b]	−0.10[b]	.33
				(0.15)	(0.08)	(0.06)	(0.05)	(0.07)	(0.49)	(0.05)	
Means and standard deviations (in parentheses) of variables				$52.88	$4.23	c	5.47	8.73	55.27	3.05	
				(5.09)	(0.96)		(1.73)	(1.79)	(1.72)	(0.97)	

[a] Coefficients of U_T for identical regression except that U_T replaces U; also given is the R^2 of the regression with U_T.

[b] Significant, with t-value greater than 1.96.

[c] Other means and standard deviations:

	$LFPR$	W
For males, aged 65 and over	29.09 (4.02)	$23.64 (4.70)
For males, aged 14–19	38.83 (7.16)	7.32 (0.57)
For single females, aged 18–19	58.67 (8.22)	17.38 (3.95)
For single females, aged 55–59	72.30 (8.10)	17.78 (3.60)

Index

* Note: The Growth of American Families survey is abbreviated as "GAF."